J B Heaton

Writing through pictures

 LONGMAN

Addison Wesley Longman Limited
Edinburgh Gate, Harlow,
Essex CM20 2JE, England
and Associated Companies throughout the world.

© Longman Group Limited 1986

First published 1986
Thirteenth impression 1996

Designed by Robert Wheeler and the
Publisher's staff
Illustrated by Ray Burrows, Jerry Collins and
Clyde Pearson.

Set in 10/11 pt Linotron Helvetica
Produced through Longman Malaysia, CL

ISBN 0-582-79108-1

Contents

Foreword to the teacher

Writing through pictures is intended for learners of English at the intermediate levels. Although the approach to writing is general in nature, writing as a means of communication is emphasised throughout and the book can be used to complement courses in both general English and English for specific purposes (ESP) by providing a wide variety of interesting and relevant topics for written work. Alternatively, *Writing through pictures* can be used to prepare students for the later, more specialised kinds of writing assignments found in ESP courses. An attempt is made, however, to provide writing tasks as similar as possible to those which most students will encounter in everyday life both inside and outside the classroom. Such tasks include the writing of factual accounts, descriptions, reports, letters and narratives, and students are given a sense of purpose for writing from the very outset. Successful writing should be seen not only as the mastery of the correct forms of the written language but also as the ability to use the written language appropriately for specific situations and readers.

The students are given three parallel tasks in each unit, progressing from *controlled* writing to *free* writing. The first task is usually presented in the form of a controlled written exercise (e.g. completing sentences, choosing suitable words, rearranging sentences, making certain changes and writing out notes in full). The finished exercise then forms a piece of continuous text which can be used as a model for the writing required for the second task. The third task allows the student to exploit what has been learnt by producing a piece of free writing. A list of appropriate vocabulary and a series of questions about the pictures are also given as a means of preparing students for the free writing exercises which follow. Teachers may also wish to identify and revise certain sentence structures and grammatical items useful for the writing task. In every case, however, students should be encouraged to check closely with the controlled writing model both before and during the free writing.

With slightly less proficient students, or with students at the lower intermediate level, it may be necessary for the teacher to revise and teach the appropriate vocabulary for the first part of each unit (i.e. the controlled writing exercise). He/She should then ask suitable questions (similar to those given for the second part of the unit) about the pictures before students start the controlled writing. Afterwards, students may be asked to close their books and engage in the second writing exercise in each unit, eventually comparing their own writing with the model. Similarly, additional preparatory work for the second part of the unit can be given – though in this case it will take the form of a controlled writing exercise along the lines of those used for the first parts of the units. If the third writing exercise proves too difficult for less proficient students, the teacher may prepare by doing the writing task in class, using students' oral answers to build up a continuous text on the blackboard.

The topics themselves comprise five broad categories: people, places, events, objects and processes. A list of these topic areas is provided in the Index for teachers who may wish to arrange their work according to these categories or to concentrate on one particular category.

Unit 1 Describing faces

1 Jeremy Field

2 Mr Carlson

3 Linda Short

4 David Robinson

5 Penny Green

6 Mr Cage

Vocabulary

Face shape:	thin, long, angular, round, baby-face(d)
Nose:	flat, pointed
Cheeks:	high cheek bones
Eyes:	small, large, narrow, round, blue etc.; twinkle, shine
Complexion:	dark, fair, smooth, rough, swarthy, weather-beaten
Hair:	blonde, (light/dark) brown, red, ginger, auburn, black, grey, white, wavy, curly, frizzy, straight, long, short, bald, balding (= becoming bald)

Connectives

and, as well as

Descriptions

Read these descriptions. Which person is being described in each paragraph?

A He has a long, angular face and a pointed nose. He has a small moustache and short black hair. His eyes are small and he wears glasses. He has a faint scar on his left cheek. He looks very serious.

B She has a round face with high cheek bones and a rather flat nose. She has wavy blonde hair and a fair complexion. Her eyes are large and she has a pleasant smile. She is a very attractive person.

C He has a weather-beaten face with red cheeks and a big nose. He has a thick beard as well as thick hair. His eyes twinkle and he usually has a big smile. He seems a jolly man.

Questions

Answer these questions about the three remaining pictures.

a) What kind of face has each person?
b) What kind of nose has he/she?
c) What kind of hair has he/she?
d) Has he/she large or small eyes?
e) Has he/she any other distinguishing marks?
f) Does he/she usually smile or look serious?
g) What kind of a person do you think he/she is?

Writing: 1

Write a short paragraph about each of the three remaining people.

Writing: 2

Now write a short paragraph describing your friend's face. What kind of a face has he/she? What about his/her hair, nose and eyes? Has he/she any distinguishing marks? What kind of a person is he/she?

5

Unit 2 Describing scenes

Standish Bay
3rd August

Dear Susan,

We are having a lovely holiday ___1___ Standish Bay. We are staying ___2___ a small house only a few yards ___3___ the beach. The scene ___4___ the window ___5___ the lounge is very beautiful and peaceful. In ___6___ of the house there is a yard ___7___ some chairs, a table and a few small trees. Just ___8___ the yard are miles ___9___ golden sand. Fortunately, there are only a few people ___10___ the beach, and so there isn't much noise. I can see a couple sunbathing ___11___ while their children are playing quietly ___12___ them. On my ___13___ there is a hill, which I hope to climb tomorrow. I can see a footpath leading ___14___ it, and so it should be quite safe. A few people are swimming ___15___ the sea, and a woman is watching a man diving ___16___ a small raft in the ___17___ of the bay. The sea is very calm today and a few yachts are visible a long distance ___18___ the shore. It is so relaxing to sit here and gaze ___19___ the view. I went swimming earlier this morning, and this afternoon we are going to hire a yacht ___20___ a few hours. I wish you were here.

Love,

Mary

Description

Mary has written a letter to a friend about her holiday. Rewrite the letter, using the best word from the box below to replace each blank. You must use each word at least once. Write your own address and the date. Change *Susan* to the name of one of your friends and use your own name at the end of the letter.

in	of	on	off	from	with	through	nearby
for	up	at	beyond	behind	right	front	middle

Connectives

while, and (so), which

Questions

Answer these questions about the picture on this page.

a) What can you see in the foreground?
b) Where is the child's swing?
c) What is the man doing while the child is sitting on the swing?
d) What is there beyond the garden on the left?
e) Whereabouts is the large wood?
f) What can you see in the distance?
g) What is there half-way up the hill on the right?
h) What are some people doing while the others are playing golf?
i) What would you do if you were on holiday here?
j) How do you think you would find the setting? (Noisy? Restful?)

Writing: 1

Imagine you are spending a holiday in the place illustrated on this page. Describe the scene and write a short account of what you are doing.

Writing: 2

Where did you last spend your holiday? Write a letter to one of your friends, describing the scene from the window of the place where you stayed. Remember to describe details in the foreground before proceeding to describe the background.

Vocabulary

at the { top / bottom } of   in the { centre / middle } of

behind, in front of, between, beyond
view, scene, scenery, landscape
beautiful, attractive, picturesque, magnificent
peaceful, relaxing, restful
yard, garden, field, golf course, mountain, waterfall

on the { left / right } of   in the { foreground / background }

opposite
adjacent } to   near, nearby, a { short / long } distance from, far from
next

7

94 Orchard Road
Colchester
9th October

Dear Charles,

I am very sorry I cannot come to meet you at the airport since I have to take my mother home from hospital at that time. Our neighbour (Peter Lee/Mrs Shaw/Miss Wilson) has kindly offered to meet you and bring you home. As you have never met (him/her) before, I shall describe (him/her) to you.

(Peter Lee/Mrs Shaw/Miss Wilson) is (tall/short/of average height) and (slim/stocky/of medium build). (He/She) is (a young/an old/a middle-aged) (man/woman) in (his/her) (early twenties/late thirties/mid-sixties) with (frizzy/wavy/long) hair and a (fair/dark/swarthy) complexion. (He/She) has (a round/an angular/an attractive) face and appears (cheerful/kind/suspicious) by nature. It is easy to recognise (him/her) because (he/she) is usually (well-/sloppily/smartly) dressed in (old jeans and a T-shirt/a jumper and slacks/a matching blouse and skirt) and wears (high-heeled shoes/flat shoes/boots).

I do hope you manage to recognise my neighbour without any difficulty and I look forward to seeing you when (he/she) brings you to my flat.

Yours sincerely,

Eddie Low

1 Peter Lee

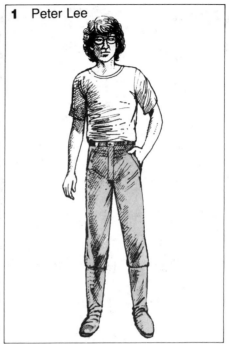

2 Mrs Shaw

3 Miss Wilson

Descriptions

Use the letter on the left to write separate letters about the people in the pictures on this page. Write **one** letter about Peter Lee, **one** letter about Mrs Shaw and **one** letter about Miss Wilson. Choose the best words in the brackets.

4 John Laker

5 Mrs Dixon

6 Mr Ashby

Vocabulary

Height: tall, short, small, of medium/average height

Build: slim/slender (women only), thin, of medium/average build, well-built, stout, stocky, fat, athletic in build

a { lovely / good / well-proportioned } figure

Age: young, middle-aged, elderly, old

in his/her { early / mid- / late } { teens / twenties / thirties etc. }

Nature: determined, serious, stern, strict, tolerant, happy-go-lucky, carefree, happy, jolly, cheerful, kind, patient, gentle, mean, cruel, understanding, impatient, suspicious

Clothes: untidy, sloppy, neat, smart,

{ untidily / sloppily / well- / neatly / smartly } dressed

jeans, trousers, shorts, blouse, shirt, jumper, sweater, cardigan, skirt, dress, (sports) coat, jacket, suit

Shoes: high-heeled shoes, flat shoes, sandals, plimsolls, boots

Connectives

since, as, because (of), and

Questions

Answer these questions about the pictures above.

a) How tall is each person?
b) What is he/she like in build?
c) How old do you think he/she is?
d) What is his/her hair like?
e) What kind of a face has he/she?
f) What can you gather about his/her nature?
g) How is he/she dressed?

Writing: 1

Write a short description of one of the three people in the pictures above.

Writing: 2

You have been asked to meet a visitor whom you have never seen before. Write a short letter to him, arranging a time and place to meet. In your letter you should describe briefly what you look like and how you will be dressed. What else can you do to ensure that the visitor will be able to identify you?

Unit 4 Describing routines

Mr Flint

Mrs Flint

Kim, Joe and May

Description

Paragraphs A to D describe a day in the life of this farming family. The sentences within each paragraph are out of order. Rewrite each paragraph, putting the sentences in the correct order according to the pictures above.

A
- He begins work at half-past six every morning as soon as it is light.
- After breakfast, Mr Flint leaves home to work in the fields nearby.
- He then spends the first part of the morning feeding his calves, and at about nine o'clock he begins to plough the fields with a small, modern tractor.
- Mr and Mrs Flint get up at quarter to six in the morning, and Mrs Flint makes breakfast for her husband.

B
- At eight-thirty they set off for school, which is over two miles away.
- They travel to school by bus every day.
- Mr and Mrs Flint's three children get up at half-past seven every morning, have their breakfast and then help their mother to wash up.

C
- She works very hard in the fields until four o'clock.
- As soon as the children have left, Mrs Flint feeds the hens and picks up the eggs which they have laid.
- Then she has lunch with him before helping him to work on the farm.
- She makes some tea and sandwiches for her husband.

D
- Kim, Joe and May go to bed at nine o'clock, and their parents go to bed an hour and a half later.
- Mr Flint returns home at six o'clock, and the family have their evening meal half-an-hour later.
- When Mrs Flint returns home, her three children help her to prepare the evening meal.
- After the meal, Mr Flint plants some vegetables, while the children do their homework.

11

Mr Lee

Mrs Lee

Janet and Dave

Vocabulary

get up, have breakfast/lunch/dinner, set off, leave, arrive, return
go by train/car, go shopping, go to work/school/the office, go home, go to bed
get a lift, take, relax, watch television, sew, help
factory, factory-worker, foreman, supervisor
office, office-worker, typist, secretary
school, playground, teacher, pupil, student, homework

Connectives

as soon as, when, after, before, then

Questions

Answer these questions about the pictures.

a) At what time do Mr and Mrs Lee get up?
b) What does Mr Lee do first when he gets up?
c) When do the Lee family have breakfast?
d) Where does Mr Lee work? How does he get there?
e) How do Janet and Dave get to school?
f) What does Mrs Lee do as soon as she arrives at work?
g) What does Mrs Lee often do in the afternoon?
h) What do Janet and Dave usually do as soon as school has finished?
i) What does everyone in the Lee family do at half-past six?
j) What does Mr Lee sometimes do in the evening?
k) How does Mrs Lee often pass the time?
l) At what time do they go to bed?

Writing: 1

Write a short account of a typical day in the lives of the members of the Lee family. Describe what they do in a similar way to the completed exercise on Page 11.

Writing: 2

Now write a short account of a typical day in your life and in the lives of members of your family.

Unit 5 Keeping a diary

1 Saturday

2 Sunday

3 Monday

4 Tuesday

14 **5** Wednesday

6 Thursday

7 Friday

8 Saturday

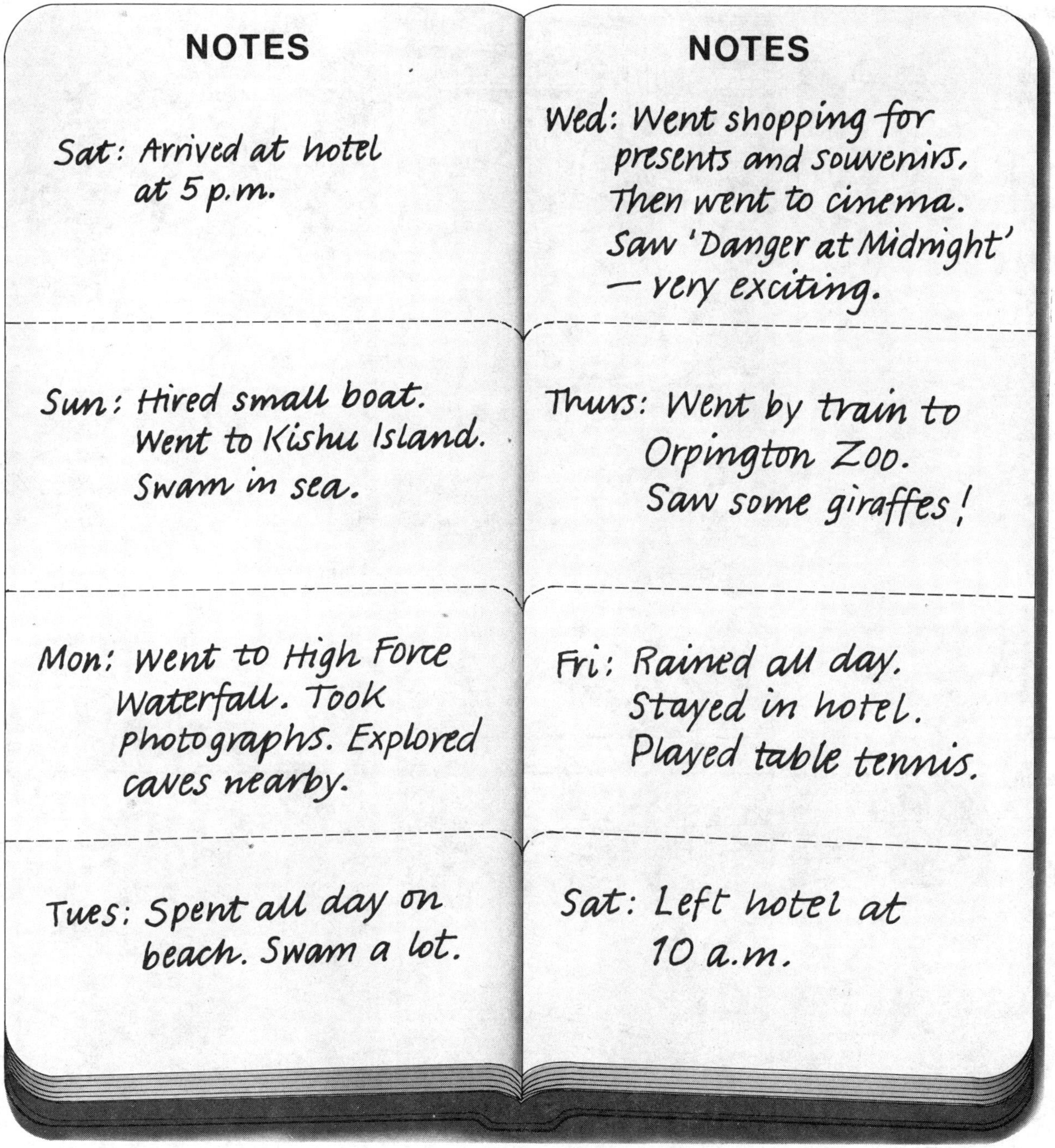

NOTES

Sat: Arrived at hotel
at 5 p.m.

Sun: Hired small boat.
Went to Kishu Island.
Swam in sea.

Mon: Went to High Force
Waterfall. Took
photographs. Explored
caves nearby.

Tues: Spent all day on
beach. Swam a lot.

NOTES

Wed: Went shopping for
presents and souvenirs.
Then went to cinema.
Saw 'Danger at Midnight'
— very exciting.

Thurs: Went by train to
Orpington Zoo.
Saw some giraffes!

Fri: Rained all day.
Stayed in hotel.
Played table tennis.

Sat: Left hotel at
10 a.m.

Writing notes in full

In the pictures you can see what Margaret did on her holiday with her parents and her two brothers. On the left is an extract from her diary.

Write out in full the notes in Margaret's diary. Begin:

We arrived at our hotel at the seaside at five o'clock on Saturday evening. The next morning my father hired a small boat, and we all went to Kishu Island, where I swam in the sea. On Monday we all set off early for . . . .

1 Tuesday

2 Wednesday

3 Thursday

4 Friday

5 Saturday

6 Sunday

7 Monday

8 Tuesday

Vocabulary

train, carriage, station, platform
get off, walk (in file), set up (camp),

pitch ⎫
erect ⎬ a tent, take down a tent, break camp
put up ⎭

camp, camp-site, camp fire, rucksack
cliffs, pool, rocks

go ⎰ fishing
⎱ shopping   borrow ⎱
⎰ cycling   hire   ⎰ a bicycle
⎱ swimming

100-metres race, high jump, long jump, sprint

Connectives

where (= and there/here), then

Questions

Answer these questions about the pictures on the opposite page.

a) What are the boys doing in Picture 1?
b) How do you think they are going to spend their holiday?
c) What are two of the boys doing in Picture 2?
d) What's the boy near the fire doing?
e) What are four of the boys buying in Picture 3?
f) What are the other two boys doing?
g) Why are the boys in their tent in Picture 4?
h) What are they doing?
i) What's happening in Picture 5?
j) Where do you think the boys are going?
k) What are the boys doing in Picture 6?
l) In Picture 7, what sports are the boys competing in?
m) What are the boys doing in Picture 8?

Writing: 1

Pretend to be **one** of the boys who went camping. Write notes for your diary about what you did. Then use the notes to write a paragraph about what you did.

Writing: 2

Try to remember everything you did one week during your last holiday from school, college or work. Write notes for your diary about what you did. Then use your notes to write a complete paragraph.

Unit 6 Writing a short story (1)

Telling a story

Joe is telling what happened when the car he was travelling in broke down on a small road in the jungle. Write out his account, replacing each blank with one word from the box.

car, Bill, broke, arms, lost, lead, However, go, walked, repair, driving, staying, path, but, men, tree, fell, until, road, talking, frightened, agree

"We were .. ¹.. along a narrow .. ².. when the car .. ³.. down. David and I wanted to go off in search of help .. ⁴.. Bill insisted on .. ⁵.. near the car. He said it was best to stay .. ⁶.. help arrived rather than .. ⁷.. in the jungle and risk getting lost. .. ⁸.., both David and I did not .. ⁹.., and David pointed to a .. ¹⁰.. which he thought would probably .. ¹¹.. to a village. We followed the path but soon we were hopelessly .. ¹².. We wandered on and on. After an hour or so we began to feel very .. ¹³.. Then David .. ¹⁴.. and cut his legs and .. ¹⁵.. I decided to climb a .. ¹⁶.. to see where we were, but it was no use. I helped David and we struggled on. Suddenly we caught sight of a .. ¹⁷.. and some .. ¹⁸.. We had .. ¹⁹.. in a circle and had returned to the car! .. ²⁰.. was standing at the side of the car, .. ²¹.. to two men who were helping him to .. ²².. it."

Vocabulary

mountain (side),
rock face, cliff,
overhanging cliff

steep, vertical,
gentle (slope)

beckon, perspire,
sweat, relax

bruised, cut, exhausted,
tired, fresh

climbing { gear / equipment }

Connectives

but, however, after, then,
when, where, which

Questions

Answer these questions about the pictures
on this page.

a) Where are the three men in Picture 1?
b) What are two of them about to do?
c) What's the third man doing?
d) Do they have any climbing equipment?
e) Where do you think the path leads?
f) What's happened to one of the climbers in Picture 2?
g) Is it a difficult or an easy climb up the rock face?
h) Where's the third man in Picture 2?
i) Where's he in Picture 3?
j) Why do you think he's pointing?
k) What are the other two men doing in Picture 3?
l) How do you think the two men will get to the top?

Writing: 1

Write a short account
of what happened.

Writing: 2

Write a few paragraphs
about **one** topic:
either something you
have done which has
proved to be of no use
and was a waste of
time and effort **or** an
adventure which
happened while you
were climbing, walking
or driving in the
country.

Pocket precision clock

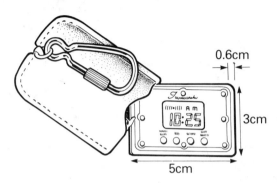

This attractive miniature clock has all the normal time functions of a digital clock. Although the clock has a stopwatch function, an alarm and a calendar, it is extremely simple to operate. The clock, which is the size of a postage stamp (5 cm × 3 cm × 0.6 cm) and extremely thin, is contained in a small leather wallet. It is attached to a silver-plated key ring so that you can always carry it with you.

Ranleigh sports cycle

This beautifully designed sports cycle weighs only 12 kilos. Although it has been made to the highest standards, with a unique 10-speed gear system, it costs only a little more than any ordinary cycle. It is ideal for anyone wishing to compete in races, tour the countryside or simply have a form of healthy exercise. It comes complete with saddlebag, front and rear light, and bell. Available in red, blue, grey or brown.

Descriptions

Read the descriptions on the left. They have been written for an advertising booklet. After reading each description, write **one** sentence giving what you think is the chief reason why someone should buy the item.

Capricorn radio cassette

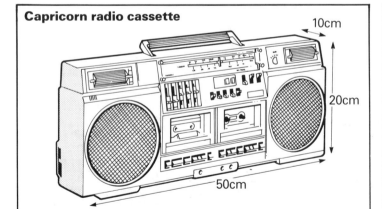

This is a compact, high quality radio cassette at an extremely reasonable price. Although it measures 50 cm × 20 cm × 10 cm, it weighs only 2 kilos, and can be easily carried. As it is suitable for use with either battery or mains, it makes an ideal portable radio cassette. Its 3-waveband radio is very powerful and offers excellent sound quality. There is a double cassette tape system which enables you to record either direct from the radio or from one cassette tape to another.

Executive briefcase

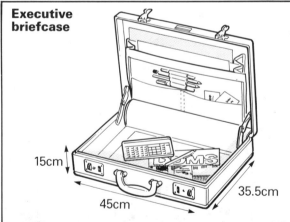

You can be the proud owner of this beautiful briefcase for a surprisingly low price. Made from real leather, the briefcase has a strong leather handle and two combination locks which you can set at any number you wish. The interior of the briefcase is lined with high quality cloth and contains three separate large pockets and a holder for four pens. It is expandable, so there is plenty of room for clothes for overnight use – though it is quite small and compact for daytime use.

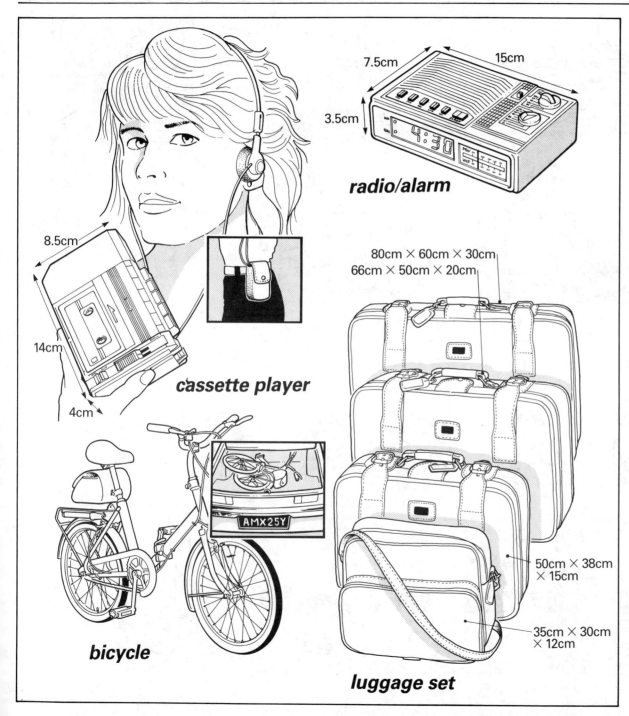

7.5cm **15cm**

3.5cm

radio/alarm

8.5cm

14cm

4cm

cassette player

AMX25Y

bicycle

80cm × 60cm × 30cm
66cm × 50cm × 20cm

50cm × 38cm × 15cm

35cm × 30cm × 12cm

luggage set

Vocabulary

Size: small, large, portable, pocket-size, thin, thick, compact
Appearance: attractive, elegant, streamlined, sleek, smart
Features: folding, collapsible, expandable
Price: (extremely) reasonable, cheap, (low) price
Quality: high/finest (quality) strong, solid
Make: make, brand, model
Materials: (made of) metal, steel, aluminium, plastic, glass, leather, cloth

Connectives

although, though, as, which, so that

Questions

Answer these questions about the pictures.

a) What is the person using to listen to the small cassette player?
b) How can you carry the cassette player?
c) Why would you (not) buy this cassette player?
d) How large is the radio/alarm clock?
e) What do you think its chief advantage is?
f) What is the chief merit of the bicycle?
g) What extra features has the cycle got?
h) Do you think the cases are attractive or not?
i) What are the measurements of the largest case?
j) What are attached to the cases?
k) What do you think the chief advantage of this set of luggage would be?

Writing: 1

Write a paragraph to accompany each picture in a shopper's catalogue.
Try to persuade people to buy each of the items.

Writing: 2

Think of any two of your possessions which you would like to sell. Describe them briefly and try to persuade people to buy them. Make your descriptions suitable for an advertisement or a notice.

Pauline Shaw

Mr Tom Shaw

Mr Peter Shaw

Mrs Mabel Shaw

Mrs Linda Green

Mr Paul Green

Helen Shaw

David Shaw

BIGGEN HOSPITAL

Pauline Shaw

Susan Shaw

Mary Green

8 Park Street
Biggen

21st February

Dear William,

I was very interested to hear that you are looking for a penfriend. I have never visited your country but I should be very happy to write to you. Let me first introduce myself. I am __1__ years old and am of __2__ height. I have __3__ hair and usually wear a __4__ and __5__. I shall try to send you a photograph of myself in my next letter.

My father works in an __6__ and my __7__ was a __8__ before she was married. I have an elder __9__, who is called Helen, and a __10__, who is David. Helen works as a __11__ and David as a doctor at __12__ Hospital. My younger __13__ is called Susan, still goes to __14__. I have a __15__ called Mary, __16__ is in the same __17__ as I am. Mary's parents live nearby, and so I often see them. I also have an uncle __18__ lives in America, and I hope to visit him next year.

I go to __19__ every day and am in Class __20__. My favourite subject is __21__, and I am very __22__ in the __23__ of __24__. I also like __25__ a lot. I hope to go to university and eventually __26__ a teacher.

My __27__ sports are __28__ and __29__. I am also keen on playing __30__ and can beat most of my friends. My other hobbies are __31__ and __32__.

Please write to me soon and tell me about yourself. I am very much looking forward to reading your letter.

Your new penfriend,

Pauline Shaw

Description

Use the information in the pictures and the family tree to complete the blanks in the letter from Pauline Shaw. Pauline is introducing herself to her new penfriend. Write out Pauline's letter, replacing each blank with one word.

Chris Hampton

Mr John Lacey

Mrs Jean Lacey

Mr Frank Hampton

Mrs Val Hampton

Lily Lacey

Harry Lacey

Karen Lacey

Thomas Hampton

Chris Hampton

Vocabulary

family tree, penfriend
elder
younger ⎫ ⎰ brother
the eldest ⎬ ⎱ sister
the youngest ⎭
parents, father, mother, uncle, aunt, cousin, relative(s), relation(s)
teacher, factory-worker, office-worker, executive, clerk, nurse,
doctor, surgeon, fireman, (garage) mechanic, typist, secretary
favourite sport(s)/game/hobby/pastime
(be) good at, like, enjoy, (be) keen on, introduce

Connectives

who, but, before, and so

Questions

Answer these questions about the pictures.

a) How old do you think Chris Hampton is?
b) How tall is he?
c) What kind of hair has he?
d) What does he usually wear?
e) What did his mother do before she was married?
f) What does his elder brother do?
g) Which of Chris's cousins is still a student at school?
h) Who works as a teacher?
i) What is Harry's job?
j) What are Chris's favourite sports?
k) What are his hobbies?

Writing: 1

Imagine you are Chris Hampton. Write a short
letter introducing yourself and your family to
Sarah Roberts, your new penfriend. Make your
letter similar to that on Page 23.

Writing: 2

Now draw a family tree for your own family. Then
write a short letter to a new penfriend, introducing
yourself and your family.

Unit 9 Describing objects

Kites

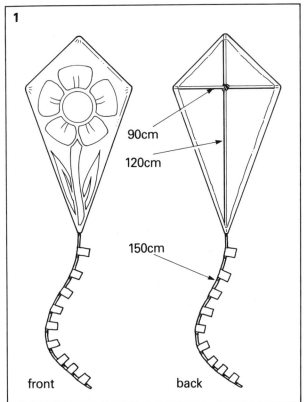

front   back

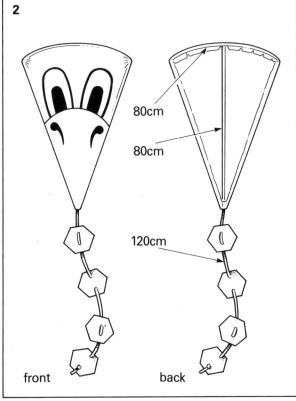

front   back

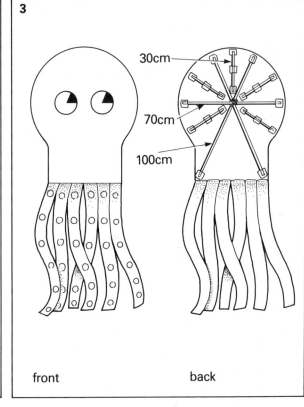

front   back

Descriptions

Write three short paragraphs about the kites above. Select sentences from each of sections A, B and C. Each paragraph should describe one kite.

A
1 The kite in the first picture is diamond-shaped.
2 The kite in the second picture is like an inverted triangle in shape, the base of which forms a slight arc.
3 The kite in the third picture is circular in shape.

B
1 Clear polythene has been used to cover the kite, which resembles a bird with a huge beak.

2 The light cloth covering the frame resembles the head of an octopus.
3 The frame is covered with wrapping paper, on which a flower has been painted.

C
1 Two sticks measuring 100 cm in length, and one stick measuring 70 cm, form the main frame.
2 The frame consists of a thin horizontal stick 90 cm long and a vertical stick 120 cm long.
3 Only two 80-cm sticks are used to form the frame: a vertical piece and a slightly bent, horizontal piece.

D
1 Four small pieces of paper, each hexagonal in shape, are attached to the tail of the kite, which is about 120 cm long.
2 Although the kite has no tail, six pieces of ribbon resembling the tentacles of an octopus are attached to its base.
3 Attached to the 150-cm-long tail are nine small rectangular pieces of paper, which flutter in the breeze like small flags.

26

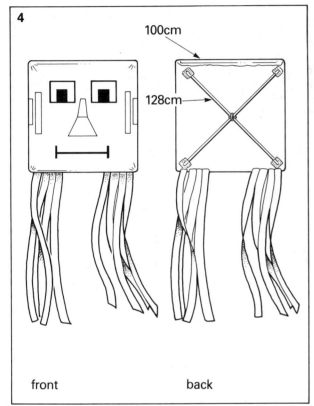

front   back

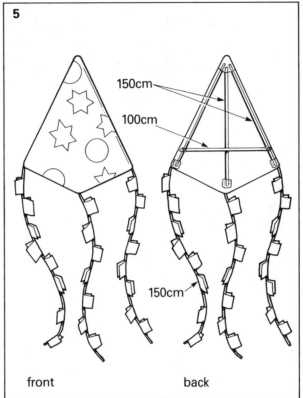

front   back

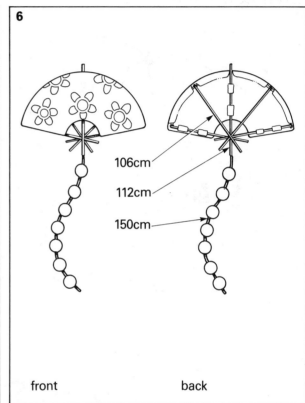

front   back

Vocabulary

Shape: round, circular, square, rectangular, long and thin (in shape), diamond-shaped, pear-shaped, egg-shaped
(shaped) like a cube/a pyramid/a box/an inverted triangle/an octopus/a fan/an aeroplane
Size: small, tiny, minute, huge, large, big, enormous, gigantic
eighty centimetres in length/in width/in height/long/wide/high
Materials: (made of) cotton/paper/plastic

Connectives

(of/on) which, although

Questions

Answer these questions about the three remaining pictures.

a) What shape is the kite in Picture 4?
b) Which kite is shaped like a fan?
c) What does the kite in Picture 4 resemble?
d) What's painted on the body of the kite in Picture 5?
e) How long are the sticks which form the frame of the kite in Picture 5?
f) How many sticks are used to form the frame of the robot kite?
g) How long is the tail of the kite in Picture 6?
h) Which kite has three tails?
i) On which kite are there circles attached to the tail?

j) Which kite on this page has the largest number of sticks?

Writing: 1

Write a short paragraph about each of the three kites on this page.

Writing: 2

Now design your own kite. First draw it and then describe the shape of the kite, the materials from which it is made, its size, and its tail.

Unit 10 Comparing places

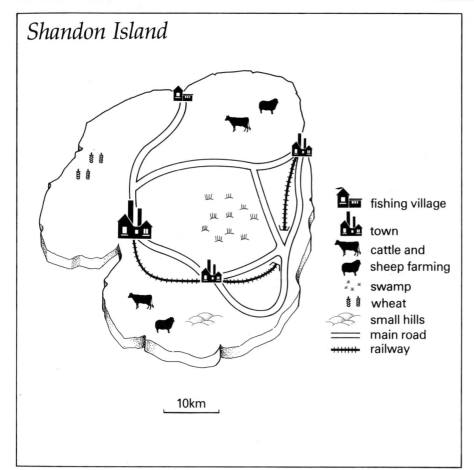

Shandon Island

Legend:
- fishing village
- town
- cattle and sheep farming
- swamp
- wheat
- small hills
- main road
- railway

10km

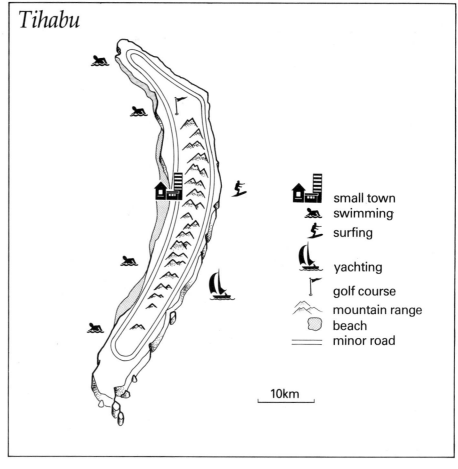

Tihabu

Legend:
- small town
- swimming
- surfing
- yachting
- golf course
- mountain range
- beach
- minor road

10km

Comparison

Write out the following paragraph, choosing the best word in the brackets.
The completed paragraph should compare Shandon Island with Tihabu.

Shandon Island is much (larger/thicker/fatter) than Tihabu. It is roughly (circular/round/spherical) in shape (although/even/whereas) Tihabu is shaped (like/as/the same) a boomerang. Wheat is (grown/farmed/made) in the (east/west/south) part of Shandon Island and there is considerable dairy farming in both (the east and the west/the north and the south). Shandon Island, moreover, has three large (urban/factory/industrial) towns, (separated/linked/chained) by road and (train/rail/line). There is also a small (fish/fishing/fisher) village on the north (edge/part/coast), connected (by/with/to) road to the largest of the towns. Tihabu, (on the other hand/on the contrary/on the opposite), has only one small town, which is a holiday (recreation/resort/residence). There is no (factory/industry/work) on the island and only one road, (which/it/this) runs (along/between/among) the coast, providing easy (access/arrival/reach) to the island's magnificent (shores/beaches/seasides) on the (east/west/south) coast. On the (east/west/north) coast of Tihabu there is excellent surfing and also (boating/sailing/shipping). (Unlike/Different from/Contrary to) Shandon Island, the (middle/central/average) part of Tihabu is quite mountainous. Whereas most of Shandon Island's income (comes from/is obtained by/arises from) industry and agriculture, Tihabu derives most of its income from (holidays/recreation/tourism).

28

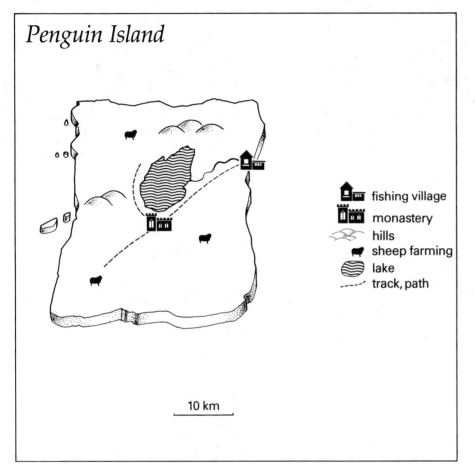

Penguin Island

fishing village
monastery
hills
sheep farming
lake
---- track, path

10 km

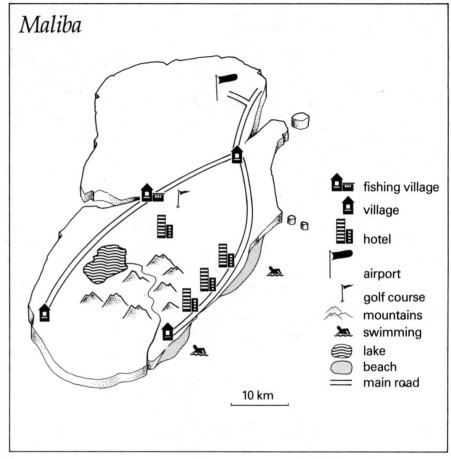

Maliba

fishing village
village
hotel
airport
golf course
mountains
swimming
lake
beach
== main road

10 km

Vocabulary

circular, oval, square, rectangular (in shape),
crescent-shaped, etc.
rural, agricultural, farming, urban, industrial
(holiday) resort, (luxury) hotel
mountainous, hilly, flat, rocky
coast(-line), shore, beach
sparsely
densely } populated

in ┐
to ┘ the { north / south / east / west } of   on the { north / south / east / west } coast of

Connectives

on the other hand, unlike, moreover, which, *-ing
forms*, whereas

Questions

Answer these questions about Penguin Island and
Maliba.

a) Are the two islands approximately the same or
    different in size?
b) How do the two islands differ in shape?
c) How many villages are there on Penguin Island?
d) How are the villages on Maliba linked?
e) How is it possible to reach Maliba?
f) Why do you think people visit Maliba?
g) Which island is the more sparsely populated?
h) What do both islands have in common?
i) Which island has mountains?
j) How do you think most people on the islands
    are able to make a living?

Writing: 1

Write a paragraph
comparing Penguin
Island and Maliba.

Writing: 2

Compare the region or
the country where you
live with a neighbouring
region or country.

29

How to make omelettes

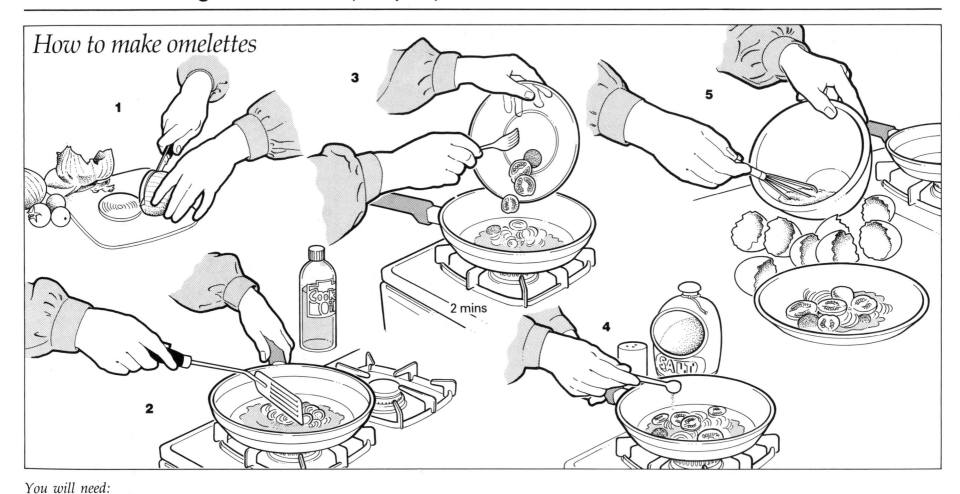

1

2

3

2 mins

4

5

You will need:

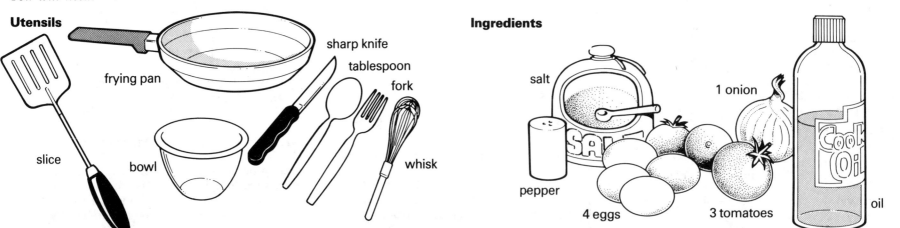

Utensils

slice

frying pan

bowl

sharp knife

tablespoon

fork

whisk

Ingredients

salt

pepper

4 eggs

1 onion

3 tomatoes

oil

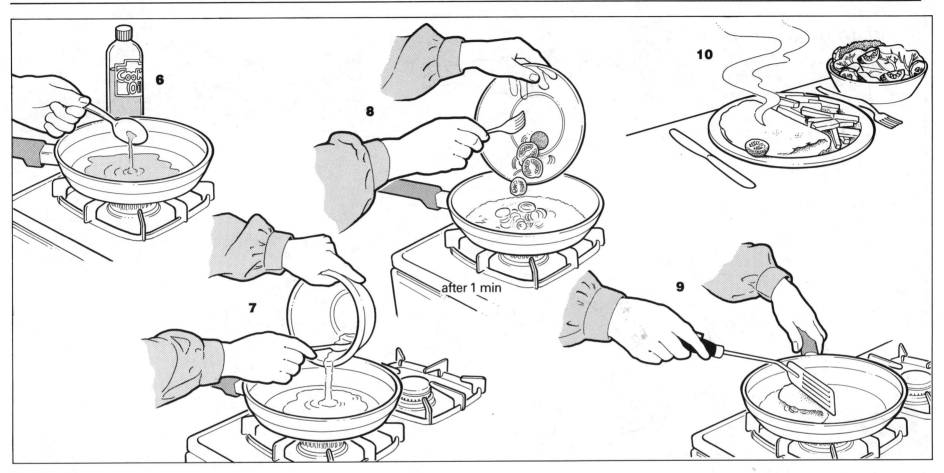

Writing a recipe

The following is a recipe for making an omelette. Rewrite it, putting each verb in brackets in its correct form and replacing each blank with the name of the correct ingredient or utensil.

You will need four ..1.., three medium-sized ..2.., one ..3.., a little oil and salt and ..4... First (slice) the ..5.. and the tomatoes. Next (fry) the (slice) onion in a little ..6.. in a pan until light brown before (add) the ...7... After (fry) the ..8.. and ..9.. for about two minutes, (add) salt and pepper to taste. Then (set) aside on a plate for a few minutes. (Take) four ..10.. and (beat) them in a ..11.. with a fork or whisk for one or two minutes. (Heat) one to two ..12.. of oil in a ..13.. before (pour) the (beat) egg in. After one minute, (put) the ..14.. and ..15.. mixture in the centre. Finally (fold) the resulting omelette in half before (take) it out of the ..16.. pan and (serve) it with chips or salad.

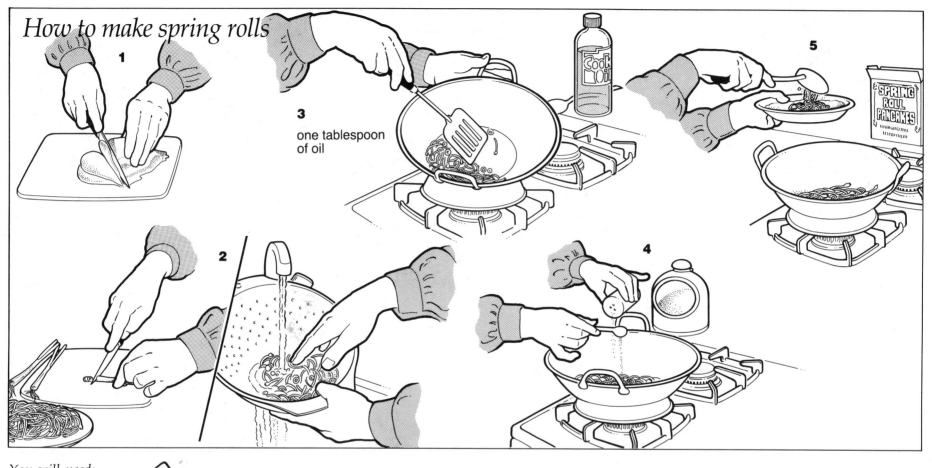

How to make spring rolls

1

2

3 one tablespoon of oil

4

5

You will need:

Utensils

slice

sharp knife   tablespoon

wok (chinese frying pan)

Ingredients

Worcester sauce

cooked chicken (6ozs)

4 sprigs of spring onions

bean sprouts (4ozs)

packet of spring roll pancakes

salt

pepper

oil

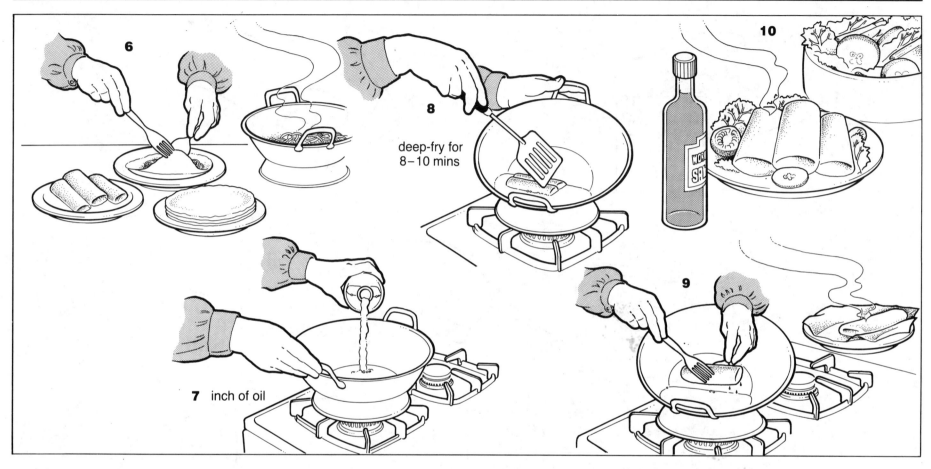

Vocabulary

ingredients: (cooked/roasted) chicken (breast),
spring onion, bean sprouts, pancake, salt, pepper,
Worcester Sauce, (sprig of) spring onion
utensils: tablespoon, frying pan (wok), slice
quantities: teaspoon, tablespoon, oz (ounce),
pinch (*n*)
packet, kitchen roll (of paper)
mixture
cook, slice, chop (up), cut (up), stir, fry, deep-fry,
spoon (*v*), fold, heat, drain, serve

Connectives

first, next, then, after (*-ing*), before (*-ing*), finally

Questions

Answer these questions about the pictures.

a) What's being sliced in Picture 1?
b) What's being done to the spring onions and
   bean sprouts in Picture 2?
c) How much oil has been put in the pan?
d) How are the ingredients being cooked?
e) What's being added in Picture 4?
f) Where are the ingredients being put in
   Picture 5?
g) What's being used to fold the pancakes?
h) What's being heated in Picture 7?
i) What's being done to the spring rolls in
   Picture 8?

j) For how long is this being done?
k) What's happening in Picture 9?
l) With what are the spring rolls being served?

Writing: 1

Write the recipe for making spring rolls.

Writing: 2

Now write a recipe for making your favourite dish.
Consult a recipe book if necessary but do not
copy any of the sentences.

Making crystals

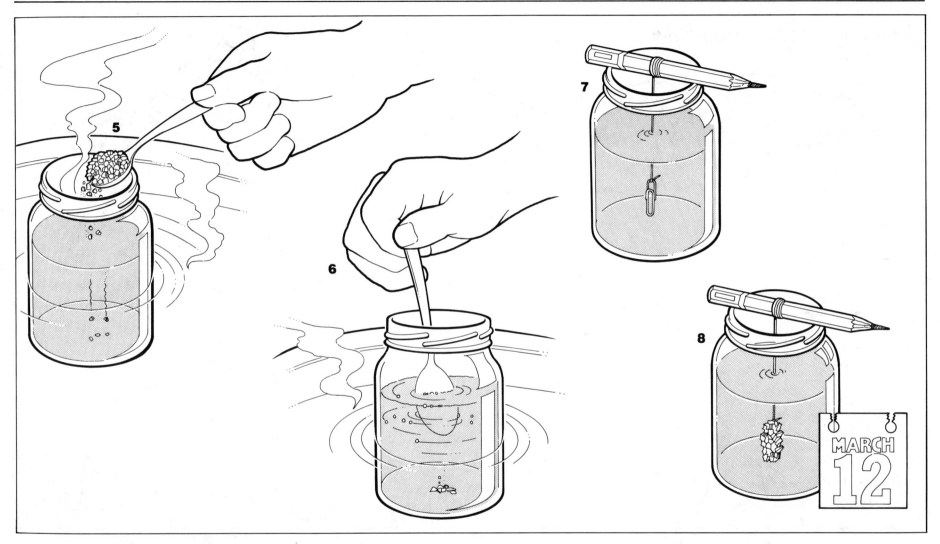

Report

Here are the instructions for performing the simple experiment illustrated. Read them carefully and imagine that you have now done the experiment as instructed. Then write a report of the experiment.

First, put a spoon inside a jar and then fill the jar with hot water. The spoon will prevent the jar from breaking as a result of the hot water. Next, add four teaspoonfuls of washing soda, stirring thoroughly until all the washing soda has dissolved. Put the jar in a bowl of very hot water in order to maintain the temperature of the solution in the jar. Add more washing soda and continue to stir after each teaspoonful has been added. Continue adding washing soda until no more will dissolve. Next, tie a paper clip onto a pencil and let the pencil rest over the jar with the paper clip suspended in the solution. The paper clip will be covered with crystals after a few days.

Begin your report of the experiment as follows:

First, a spoon was put inside a jar, which was then filled with hot water. The spoon prevented the jar from breaking as a result of the hot water. Next, four teaspoonfuls . . . .

Making a fire extinguisher

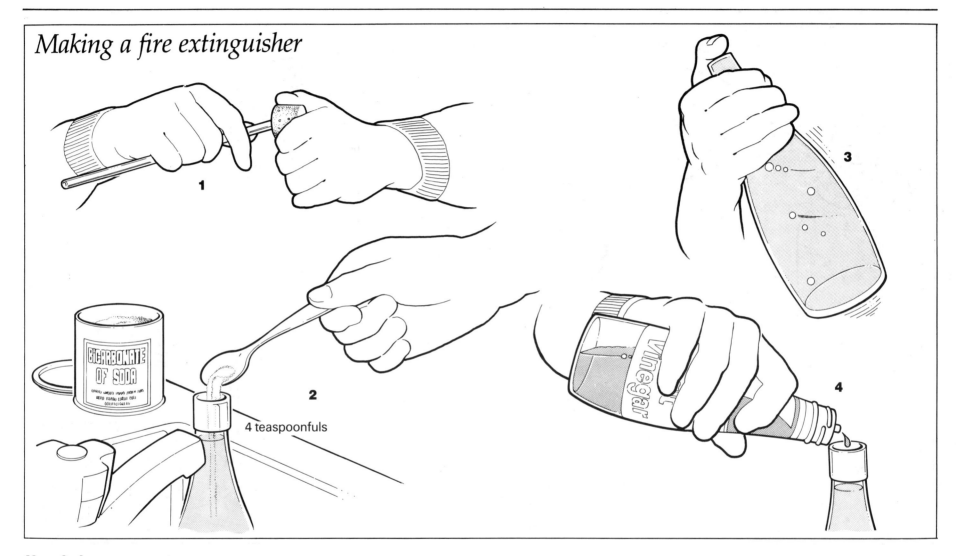

1

2

4 teaspoonfuls

3

4

Vocabulary

fire extinguisher, wine bottle, (plastic) tube, cork
baking powder (= bicarbonate of soda/sodium bicarbonate), vinegar (= acetic acid), carbon dioxide
solution
teaspoonful
insert, pour, shake, dissolve, direct (*v*), light (*v*), extinguish

Connectives

in order to, until, first, next, after

Questions

Answer these questions about the pictures.

a) What do you need for this experiment?
b) Where's the person putting the tube in Picture 1?
c) How many teaspoonfuls of bicarbonate of soda are being put in the water?
d) What's being shaken in picture 3?
e) What's next added to the solution?
f) What's happening in Picture 5?

g) What's the person doing in Picture 6?
h) Where's he doing this experiment now?
i) Why do you think he's there?
j) What's happening in Picture 7?
k) What's the bottle being used as in Picture 8?
l) What do you think has been produced by mixing bicarbonate of soda and vinegar? (Look at the vocabulary section.)

Writing: 1

Write instructions for performing this experiment. Then imagine that you have done the experiment according to the instructions you wrote. Write a report of the experiment.

Writing: 2

Can you remember any experiment which you have recently conducted? Write instructions for performing the experiment. Then write a report of the experiment.

Unit 13 Giving directions

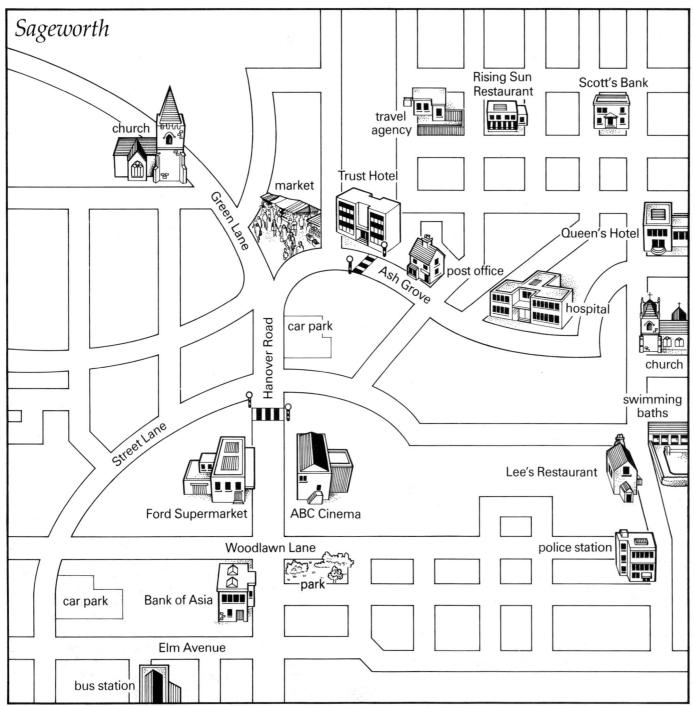

Sageworth

church

Green Lane

market

Trust Hotel

travel agency

Rising Sun Restaurant

Scott's Bank

Queen's Hotel

Ash Grove

post office

hospital

car park

church

Hanover Road

swimming baths

Street Lane

Ford Supermarket

ABC Cinema

Lee's Restaurant

Woodlawn Lane

park

police station

car park

Bank of Asia

Elm Avenue

bus station

Directions

1 Read these directions, following them on the map of Sageworth. Write the letter Z where you think the writer lives.

When you leave the bus station, turn right and walk to the junction of Elm Avenue and Hanover Road. Turn left and walk up Hanover Road, passing the Bank of Asia on your left and a small park just opposite. Cross Woodlawn Lane and continue up Hanover Road. On your left you will see the new Ford Supermarket and on your right the ABC Cinema. Cross Hanover Road at the zebra-crossing just before the Street Lane junction and keep straight on until the road forks. Then bear right and walk along Ash Grove, crossing it at the zebra crossing in front of the Trust Hotel. Take the first turning left after the hotel and walk some distance up this street. Take the fourth turning left and you will see my house at the end of the street on the right-hand side just opposite a travel agency.

2 Now direct someone back from the writer's house to the bus station. Use the paragraph above as the basis for your directions.

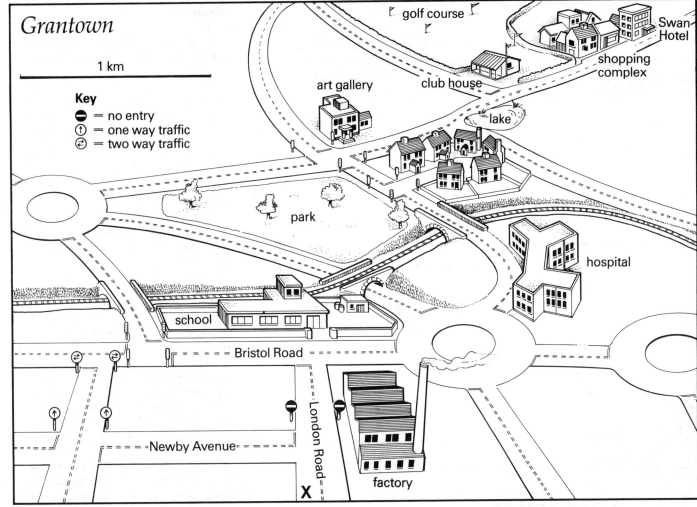

Grantown

1 km

Key
- = no entry
① = one way traffic
⇄ = two way traffic

golf course

Swan Hotel

shopping complex

club house

art gallery

lake

park

hospital

school

Bristol Road

Newby Avenue

London Road

factory

X

b) What is it necessary to do in order to reach Bristol Road?

c) How many roundabouts can you see on Bristol Road?

d) Which turning should you take at the first roundabout?

e) What will you pass on your right before the railway bridge?

f) What should you do at the first set of traffic lights?

g) What should you do at the second?

h) The road forks at the lake. Which fork should you take?

i) What is there between the club house and the hotel?

j) Approximately how far is it to the hotel from the roundabout in Bristol Road?

Writing: 1

Imagine that someone has just arrived in Grantown from London. He is driving a car and has stopped at the point marked X. He has telephoned the Swan Hotel for directions to reach the hotel. You have answered the phone. Write out the directions which you would give him.

Writing: 2

Write directions to your home from the nearest bus stop, bus station or railway station. You should write the directions so that you can read them out over the phone to someone who will visit you either on foot or by car.

Vocabulary

junction, traffic lights, roundabout, fork, no entry, one-way (street)

turn / bear { left / right }

keep { left / straight on / right }

on your { left / right }

on the { left-hand / right-hand } side (of the road)

a { left / right } turn

take the { first / second / third } { road / turning } { left / right }

Connectives

when, then, until, -ing forms

Questions

Look at the map of Grantown and trace the route from the point marked X to the Swan Hotel. Answer these questions about the route.

a) Why isn't it possible to drive straight up London Road to Bristol Road?

Unit 14 Reporting an accident

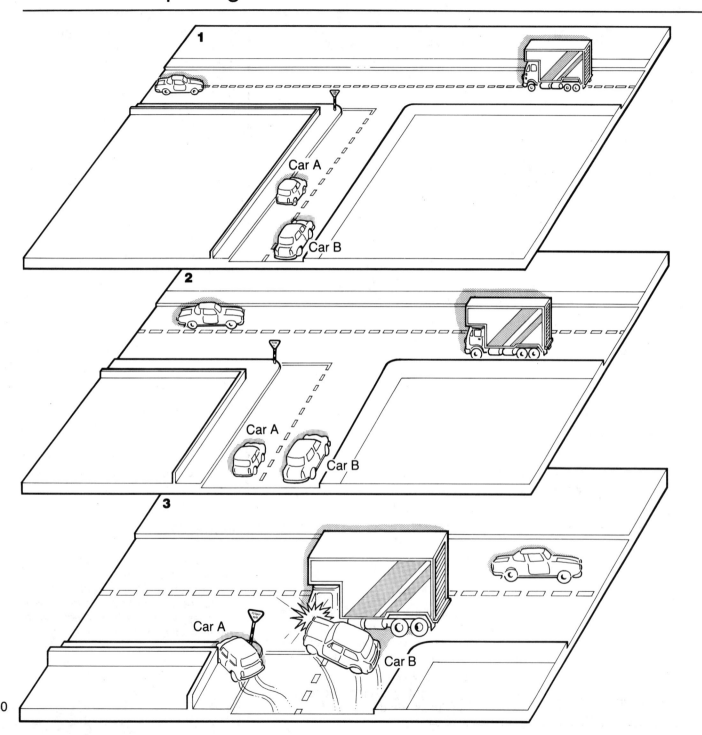

Reports

1 Read the following report of the accident shown in the pictures on the left.

I was driving down a road at about 50 km/h when the car behind began to overtake me. I slowed down, as we were approaching a fairly busy T-junction, but the car overtaking me accelerated in order to pass me. The driver suddenly seemed to notice the T-junction, but there was not time for him to slow down. At that moment a lorry was approaching the T-junction from right to left, travelling at approximately 30 km/h. The driver of the car which was overtaking me swerved to the left in order to avoid hitting the lorry. Unfortunately, this action forced me to swerve to the left and mount the pavement. I scraped the front wing of the car against a wall and hit a road sign before coming to a halt. The car was not badly damaged, however, and I was not injured in any way. Unfortunately, the driver of the car which had overtaken me hit the side of the lorry, causing considerable damage to his own car. The driver himself was also slightly injured, but fortunately the lorry driver was not hurt. The only other witness to the accident was the driver of a sports car which had been approaching the T-junction in the opposite direction to the lorry.

Who wrote this report?

2 Now imagine you are the driver of the other car. Write a similar report, but this time from **his** point of view. Use the report above as a guide.

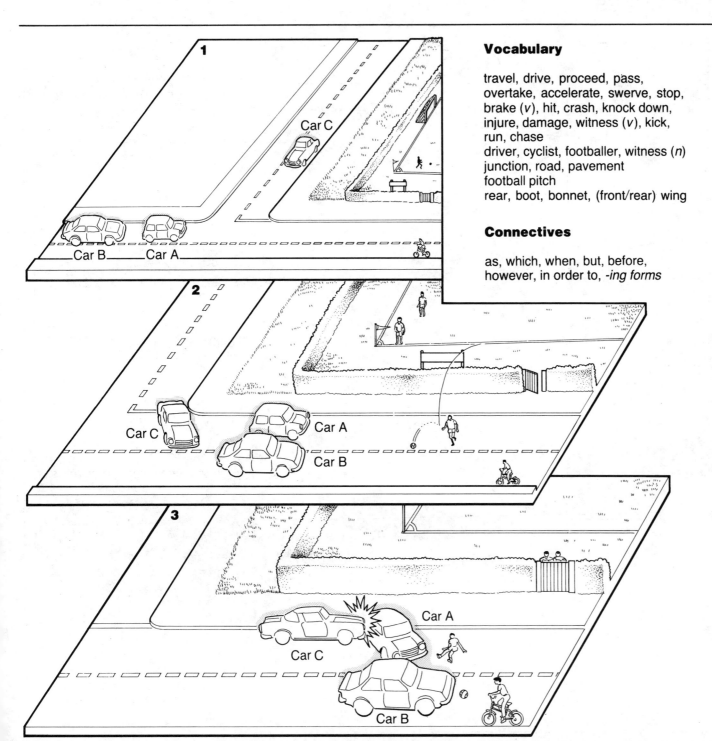

Vocabulary

travel, drive, proceed, pass,
overtake, accelerate, swerve, stop,
brake (*v*), hit, crash, knock down,
injure, damage, witness (*v*), kick,
run, chase
driver, cyclist, footballer, witness (*n*)
junction, road, pavement
football pitch
rear, boot, bonnet, (front/rear) wing

Connectives

as, which, when, but, before,
however, in order to, -*ing forms*

Questions

Answer these questions about the
accident shown in the pictures on
this page.

a) Where is Car B in the first
   picture?
b) What are all three cars
   approaching?
c) Where's the football pitch?
d) Where's Car C in the second
   picture?
e) What's Car B doing?
f) What has one of the boys just
   done?
g) What has happened in the third
   picture?
h) Which car do you think has
   suffered the worst damage?
i) Who witnessed the accident?
j) Who do you think was chiefly
   responsible for the accident?

Writing: 1

Imagine you are the cyclist. Write a
short report of the accident,
describing everything which
happened and saying who you think
caused it. Then imagine you are the
driver of Car A. Write a similar
report from your point of view.

Writing: 2

Write a brief report about any road
accident which you have seen. If
you have not seen an accident, try
to recall a time when you almost
had an accident. Then imagine that
the accident really occurred and
describe it.

Frogs

1 One frog can lay more than 1,000 eggs (= frog spawn).

2 The newly-hatched tadpoles cannot yet swim and eat.

3 after 3 weeks

eye

longer tail

mouth

gills

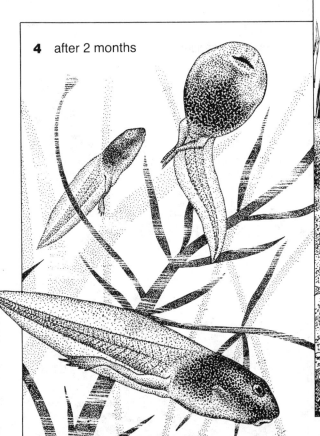

4 after 2 months

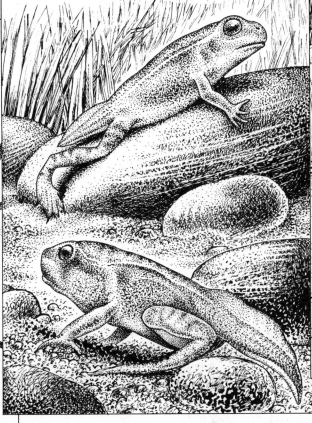

5 after 3 months lungs replace gills

6 after 3 years

Description

The following sentences about the growth of tadpoles into frogs are all out of order. Rewrite them, putting them in their correct order. (Use the pictures to help you.)

Begin your paragraph as follows:
One frog can lay more than a thousand eggs . . . .

1 These back legs grow larger while at the same time small front legs also appear.
2 Soon small tadpoles emerge from the eggs in the water.
3 During the following three weeks they develop a mouth, eyes and gills, and they also grow a much longer tail, enabling them to swim and eat.
4 Soon their tail completely disappears, and lungs replace the gills.
5 One frog can lay more than a thousand eggs.
6 At first the young tadpoles remain motionless by the side of their eggs or cling to small plants in the pond.

7 The back legs are now extremely powerful, and so the frogs can jump high in the air.
8 Ducks, for example, cannot eat the eggs because they are too slippery to hold in their beaks.
9 The tadpoles have now become small frogs.
10 The small eggs, which are always laid in water, are surrounded by a jelly-like substance to protect them.
11 As the tadpoles continue to grow, two small back legs eventually appear.

Butterflies

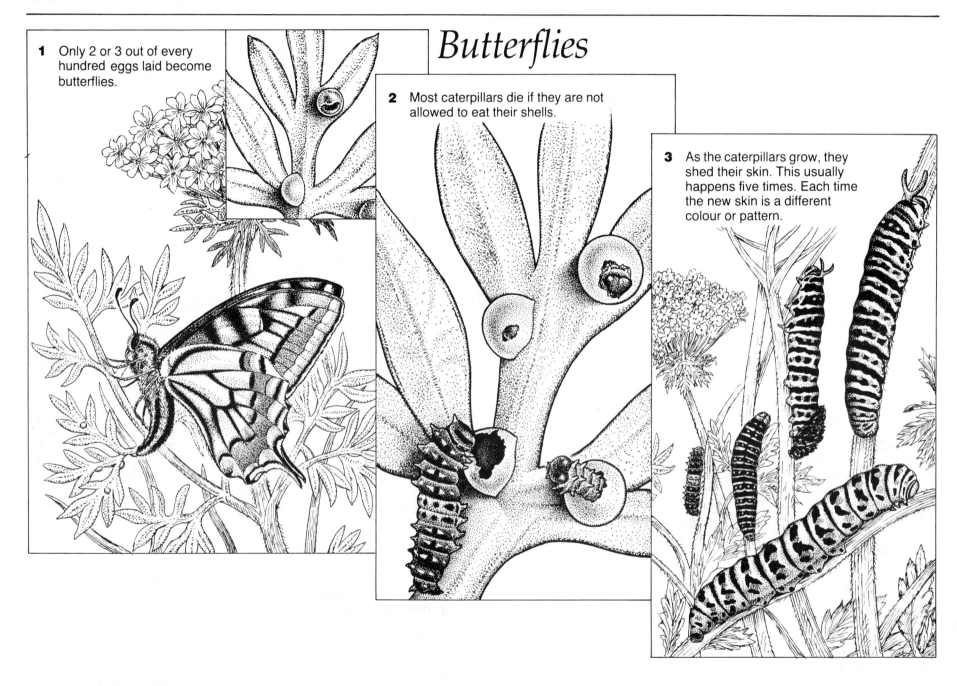

1 Only 2 or 3 out of every hundred eggs laid become butterflies.

2 Most caterpillars die if they are not allowed to eat their shells.

3 As the caterpillars grow, they shed their skin. This usually happens five times. Each time the new skin is a different colour or pattern.

4 The chrysalis stays motionless but great changes are now taking place. Inside the chrysalis, the caterpillar is developing into a butterfly.

5 The butterfly dries its wings after emerging from the chrysalis.

6 a few hours later

Vocabulary

caterpillar, larva (larvae), chrysalis (chrysales), butterfly, egg, shell
emerge, hatch (out), shed, burst (out of), split, survive, develop, become, happen, occur
change (*n*), metamorphosis
skin, colour, pattern
motionless(ly), limp(ly)

Connectives

as, while, during, at first, which, so, because, too . . . to

Questions

Answer these questions about the pictures.

a) Where are the eggs being laid in Picture 1?
b) Approximately what percentage eventually become butterflies?
c) What do the newly-hatched caterpillars look like?
d) What do they do after they have hatched?
e) What are the caterpillars doing in Picture 3?
f) About how many times do you think this happens?
g) What have the caterpillars now become in Picture 4?
h) What does the chrysalis do during this stage?
i) What is emerging in Picture 5?
j) What kind of wings do these newly-formed butterflies have?
k) What has happened to the butterflies in Picture 6?

Writing: 1

Describe briefly the growth of caterpillars into butterflies, carefully tracing each stage in their development and metamorphosis.

Writing: 2

Describe the life cycle of any insect, fish or mammal with which you are familiar.

The rain cycle

Description

Complete the sentences by choosing the right endings from the box. Your paragraph will then describe the rain cycle.

1 The evaporation of water from the sea is caused . . .
2 Although sometimes moisture condenses high in the air above the sea and falls over the sea as rain, . . .
3 As a result of the further evaporation of water from rivers and lakes, . . .
4 This moist warm air soon rises . . .
5 Eventually in the high, cold atmosphere, with less atmospheric pressure, the warm air expands . . .
6 Condensation then takes place . . .
7 When the water droplets in the clouds become large enough, . . .
8 The rain water finds its way into streams and rivers, . . .

---

more moisture collects in the air.

eventually returning to the sea and completing the cycle.

chiefly by heat from the sun, and by the wind.

and rain clouds form.

over cooler air.

they fall as rain or snow over the land, especially over the hills.

air currents carry most of the moisture over the land.

and begins to cool.

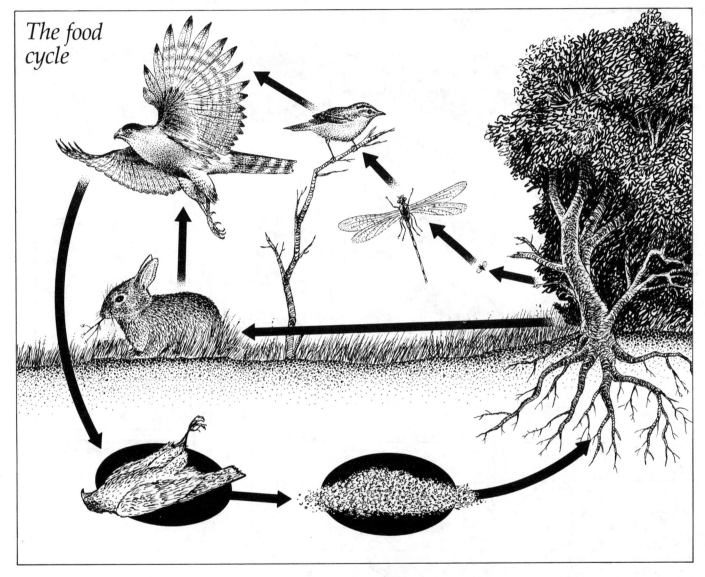

The food cycle

c) What do small birds and small animals often eat?
d) What happens to many of these small birds and animals?
e) What do all animals, birds and insects eventually do?
f) What happens to their bodies?
g) What happens as a result of the action of bacteria on the dead matter?
h) How is it then absorbed by plants and trees?
i) In what way is it useful to them?
j) What function can the plants and trees then perform?

Writing: 1

Write a short paragraph explaining the way in which the food cycle works.

Writing: 2

Write a short paragraph explaining **one** of the following cycles: the DDT cycle, the carbon cycle, the nitrogen cycle, a food chain or the pollution of seas and rivers. You may consult any reference book to help you, provided that you do not copy any sentences from the book.

Vocabulary

cycle, chain, process
in turn
plants, trees, leaves, seeds, roots
inorganic matter, dead matter,
inorganic chemicals, bacteria
bird of prey, victim, insects

eat, devour, kill, die, decay,
decompose

Connectives

as a result (of), although, when, then,
-ing forms

Questions

Answer these questions about the picture.

a) What is eaten by small insects?
b) What happens to many small insects?

Manufacturing tea

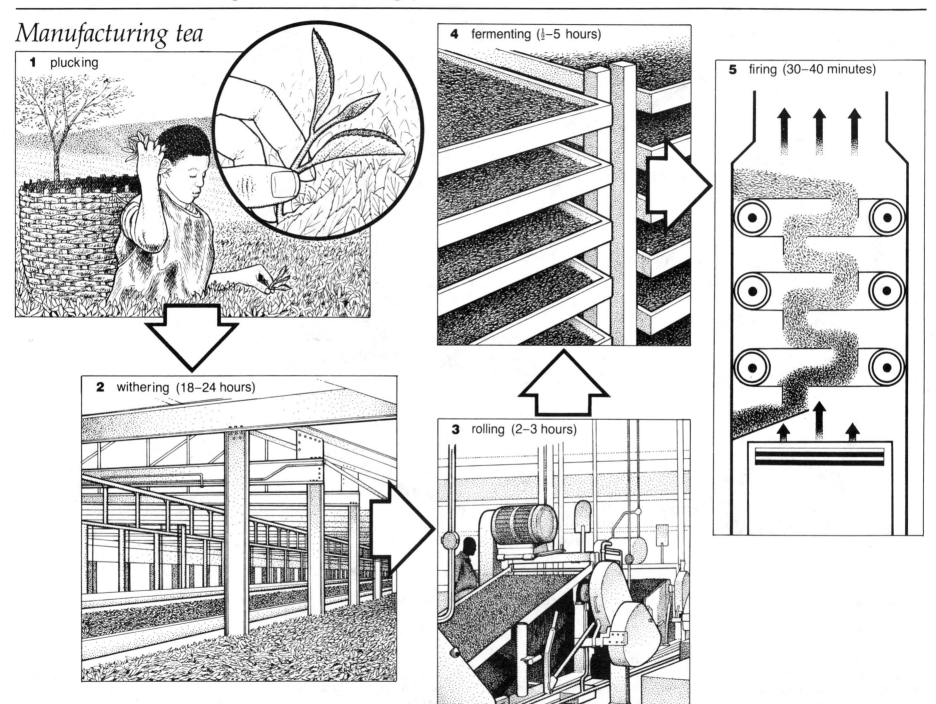

1 plucking

2 withering (18–24 hours)

3 rolling (2–3 hours)

4 fermenting (½–5 hours)

5 firing (30–40 minutes)

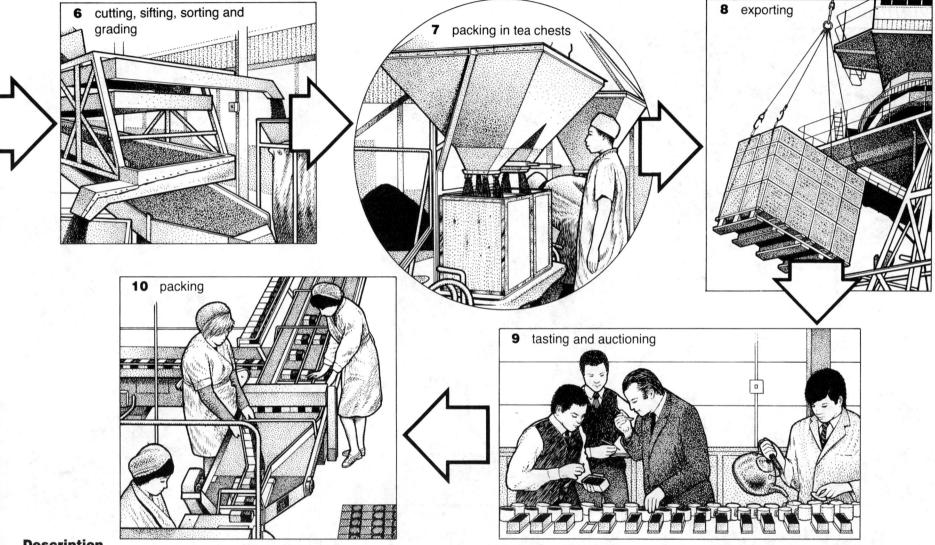

6 cutting, sifting, sorting and grading

7 packing in tea chests

8 exporting

10 packing

9 tasting and auctioning

Description

The following sentences about the manufacture of tea are out of order.
Put them in their correct order.
Use the pictures to help you.
Begin your paragraph as follows:

Only the top bud and the two leaves immediately below it are plucked from each tea plant.

1 The leaves are then allowed to ferment slightly on glass shelves for between half-an-hour and five hours.
2 Before being auctioned, the tea is tasted by experts for valuation.
3 Only the top bud and the two leaves immediately below it are plucked from each tea plant.

4 Finally, it is put in small packets and sold in shops.
5 After this, the leaves are dried for thirty or forty minutes on trays moving over a small furnace.
6 The withered leaves are then fed into a rolling machine for up to three hours in order to break up the cells and release the juices.

7 The fresh leaves are then spread on racks or shelves and allowed to wither for between eighteen and twenty-four hours.
8 After being carefully graded, the leaves are packed in large tea chests and exported.

Manufacturing coffee

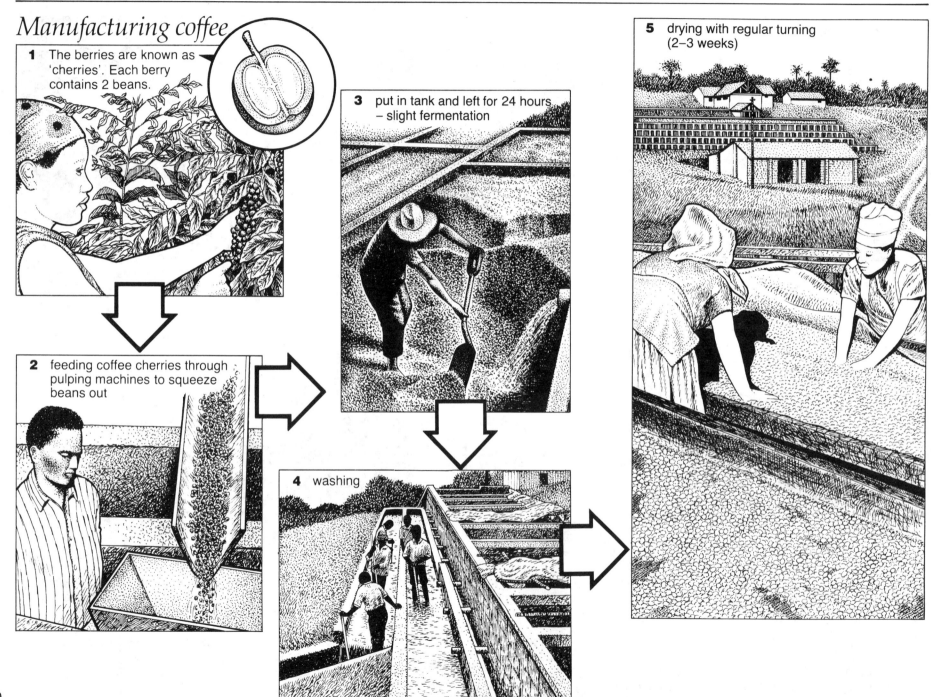

1 The berries are known as 'cherries'. Each berry contains 2 beans.

2 feeding coffee cherries through pulping machines to squeeze beans out

3 put in tank and left for 24 hours – slight fermentation

4 washing

5 drying with regular turning (2–3 weeks)

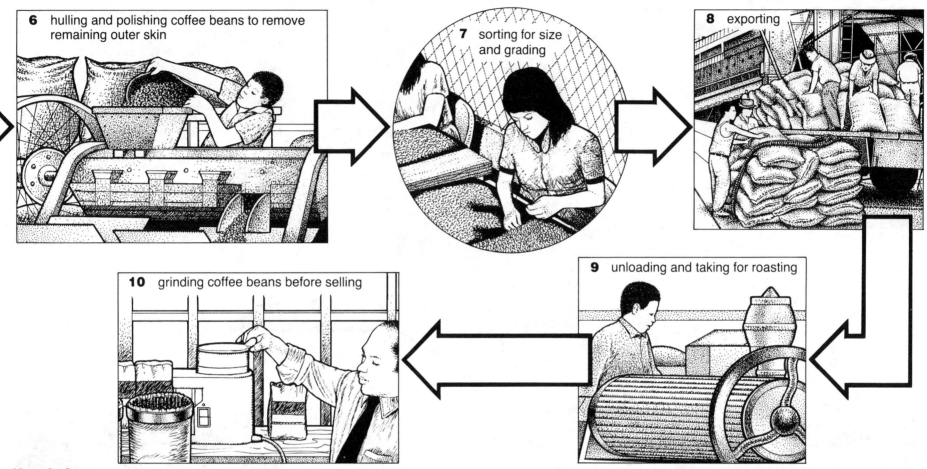

6 hulling and polishing coffee beans to remove remaining outer skin

7 sorting for size and grading

8 exporting

9 unloading and taking for roasting

10 grinding coffee beans before selling

Vocabulary

pick, pluck, feed into/through (a machine), pulp (v), squeeze, ferment, wash, spread, dry (v)
turn over, hull, polish, sort (v), grade (v), export (v), (un)load, roast, grind
berry, bean, seed, skin
pulping machine, fermentation tank, washing canal, rolling machine, revolving drum, hulling machine, roasting plant, grinder

Connectives

after (being), before (being), then, later, finally, in order to

Questions

Answer these questions about the pictures.

a) What's being picked in Picture 1?
b) How many beans or seeds are there in each berry?
c) Where are the beans being fed in Picture 2?
d) Why is this being done?
e) What's happening in Picture 3?
f) For how long are they being left there?
g) The beans are moved before fermentation can really take place. Where are they moved?
h) What's happening to the beans in Picture 5?
i) Why are some beans being turned over?
j) Why are the beans being put in a hulling machine?
k) What's happening in Picture 7?
l) What are the men doing in Picture 8?
m) What's happening to the beans in Picture 9?
n) What usually happens just before the coffee beans are finally sold?

Writing: 1

Describe briefly the manufacture of coffee, carefully tracing each stage in the processing of the beans.

Writing: 2

Now describe briefly the production and manufacture of **one** of the following: cotton, rice, rubber, sugar, steel or cloth.

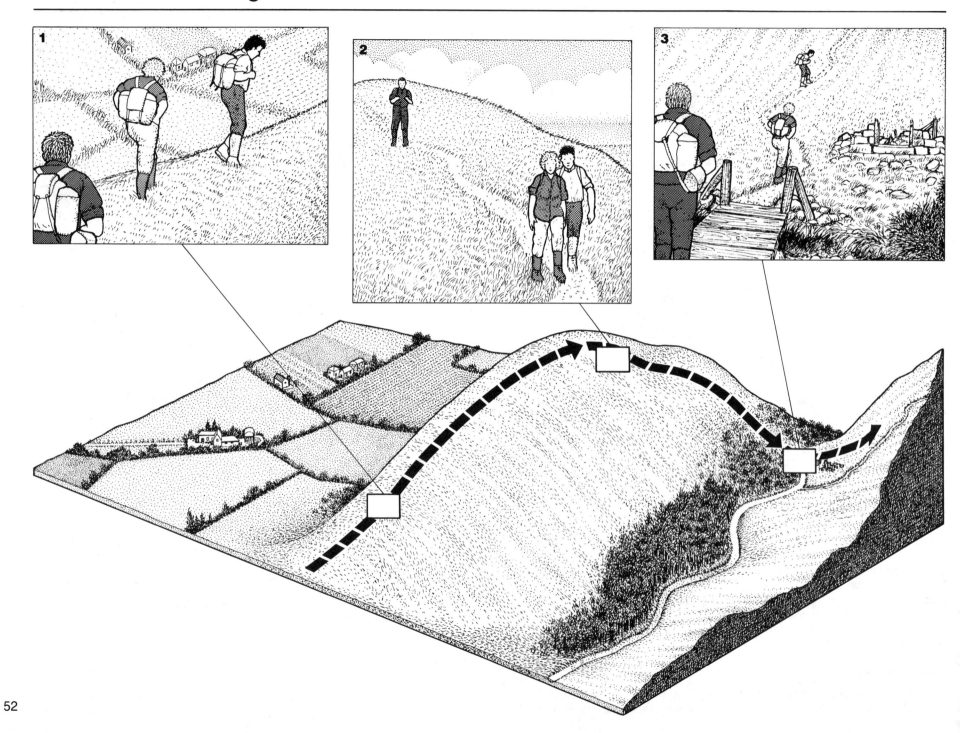

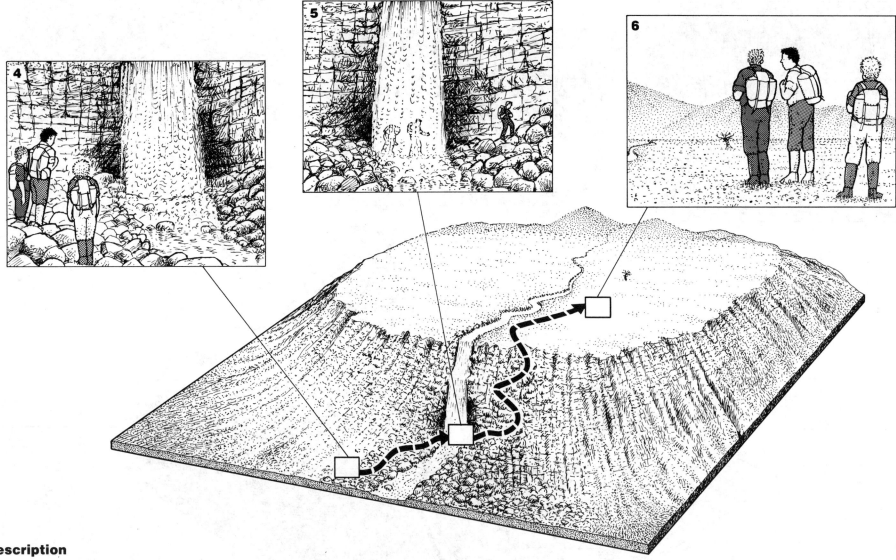

Description

Write out the following notes as complete sentences. A single oblique line (/) denotes the end of a short unit in a sentence and a double oblique line (//) denotes the end of a sentence. The completed paragraph should describe the journey illustrated in the pictures. The first sentence has been written out in full to help you start.

As we walked up the hill, we saw the land fall away on either side.//few farms scattered about wide valley on left / but no traces of buildings or fields / in narrow valley on right//continued along high ridge several miles / before descended into narrow valley on right//fewer trees in valley now / and ruins of small hut visible on other side of stream//before began climb again/

crossed narrow wooden bridge over stream// large waterfall towered above us / on other side could see route up//after walked with difficulty under waterfall / slowly climbed up rocky face//on top huge plateau / which stretched for miles// solitary tree / stunted and dwarfed / seemed emphasise desolation//in far distance possible make out / faint outline of mountain//

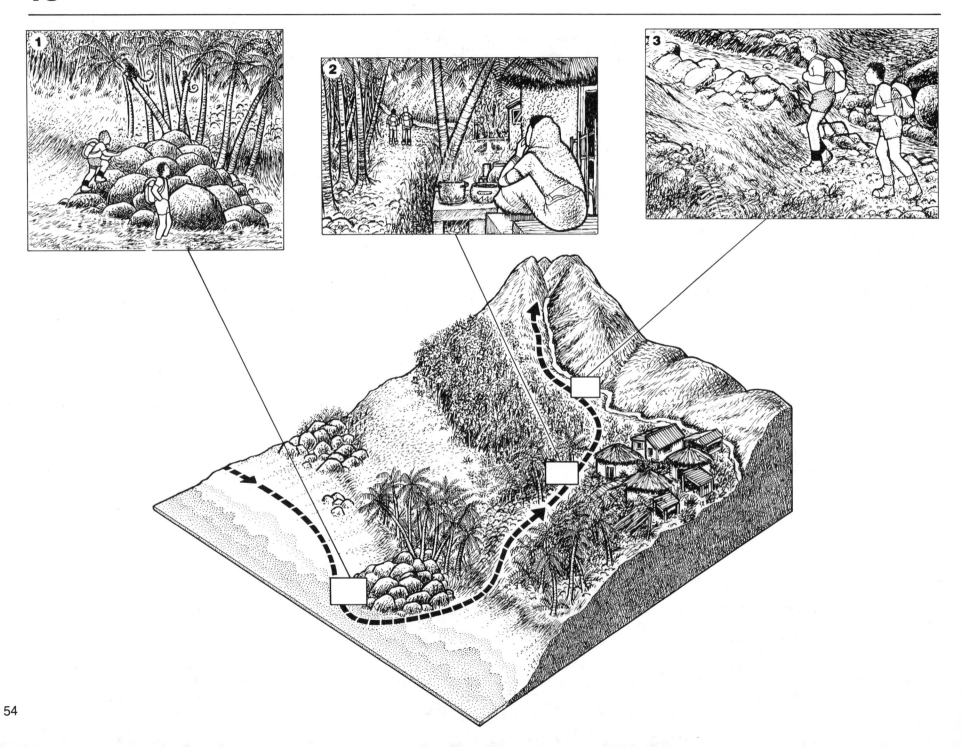

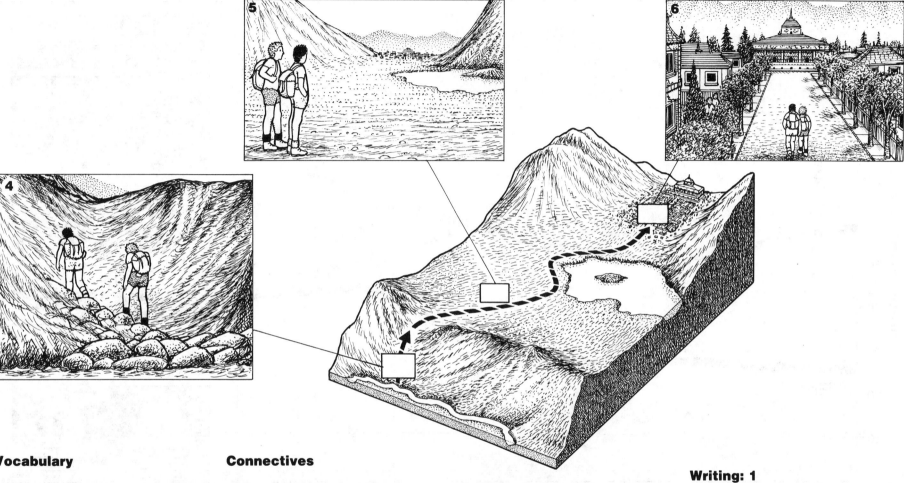

Vocabulary

seashore, valley, plateau, mountain, rocks, rocky outcrop
trees, jungle, tropical rain forest, undergrowth, bushes, scrub(land), vegetation
thick, lush, dense, sparse, barren, cultivated
upstream, downstream
hut, house, palace
route, path, (tree-lined) avenue
clear a way, come across, stumble on, reach, make for, head towards
follow⎫ ⎧a route
take ⎭ ⎩a path

Connectives

as, but, before, after, which

Questions

Answer these questions about the pictures.

a) Where were the two men in Picture 1?
b) Why was one of them walking in the sea?
c) What did they come across in the trees near the shore?
d) What was the woman doing?
e) Where did the two men make for?
f) What was the surrounding countryside like when they reached the stream?
g) What route did the men take after they had walked near the stream?
h) What did they see after they had reached the top of the valley?
i) What kind of a road led to the small town?
j) What was the town like?

Writing: 1

Write a short description of the route which the two men took to the small town.

Writing: 2

Now describe briefly **either** the route which you followed when you last went for a walk in the country, **or** the route to an interesting building or place near where you live.

Unit 19 Describing graphs

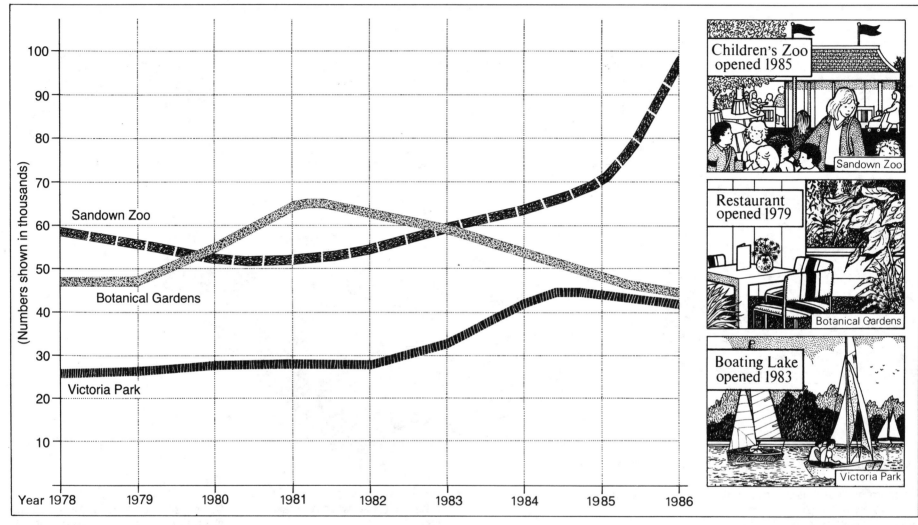

Year 1978   1979   1980   1981   1982   1983   1984   1985   1986

Description

The information in the graph above will help you to complete the following paragraph about numbers of visitors to the Botanical Gardens, Sandown Zoo and Victoria Park. Write out the paragraph, replacing each letter (X) and (Y) with an appropriate word from the list below and replacing (Z) with the correct number.

(X) decrease, fall, drop, rise, increase, climb, level off

(Y) sharp(ly), steep(ly), sudden(ly), slow(ly), slight(ly), gradual(ly), stead(il)y

The graph shows the numbers of visitors to Sandown Zoo, the Botanical Gardens and Victoria Park from 1978 to 1986. Apart from the period from 1980 to 1983, Sandown Zoo has been the most popular attraction. In 1978 almost (Z) people visited the zoo. Although this number (X) (Y) during the next 3 years, it then (X) (Y) until 1985. In this year a children's zoo was opened, resulting in a (Y) (X) from (Z) to (Z) within one year. In contrast, the number of visitors to the Botanical Gardens (X) after a restaurant had been opened in 1979, from (Z) to (Z), but then (X) (Y) to (Z) in 1986. The least popular attraction was Victoria Park, with only (Z) visitors in 1978. This number (X) only (Y) but in 1983 boating was introduced on the lake and the number of visitors (X) quite (Y). Unfortunately, however, the number (X) in 1984 and has remained (Y) since then.

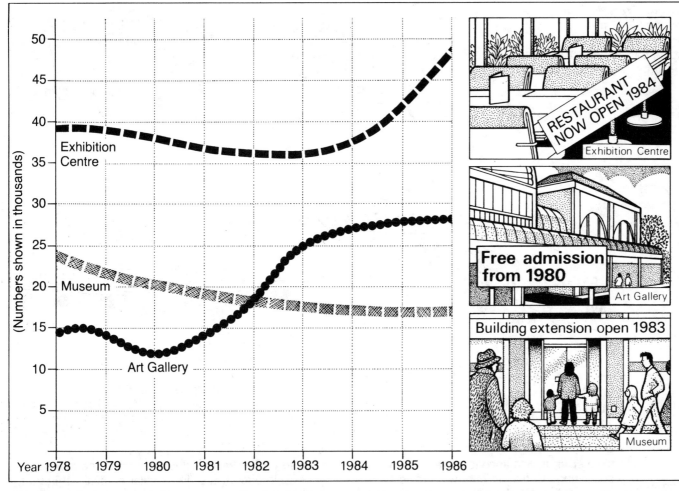

19

* Nos. in thousands

i) What happened to this number after 1983?

j) When was the number of visitors to the Art Gallery the same as the number of visitors to the Museum?

Writing: 1

Write a short description of the graph, commenting on the reasons for each increase or decrease in numbers.

Writing: 2

Here are some figures for the numbers of tourists visiting Alitonia, Brapul and Chondril from your country. Direct flights to Brapul were introduced in 1984, air fares were reduced to Chondril in 1981 and package tours to Alitonia were introduced in 1983.

Year	*Visitors to Alitonia	*Visitors to Brapul	*Visitors to Chondril
1980	54	16	69
1981	58	15	102
1982	60	19	123
1983	102	22	125
1984	110	28	130
1985	130	30	128
1986	148	29	134

Draw your own graph to show this information and then write a paragraph about the number of tourists visiting the three countries.

Vocabulary

art gallery, exhibition centre, museum, extension, restaurant
free admission, opening, visitor, attraction
popular
decrease, fall, drop, increase, rise, climb, level off
less (than), more (than), the same as
sharp, sharply, steep, steeply, sudden, suddenly, slow, slowly, slight, slightly, gradual, gradually, steady, steadily

Connectives

in contrast, however, but, although, then, after, apart from, -ing forms

Questions

Answer these questions about the graph above.

a) Which places does the graph give information about?

b) What is the most popular attraction?

c) What was the number of visitors there at the beginning of 1986?

d) Why did the number suddenly increase in 1984?

e) What was the least popular attraction in 1978?

f) What happened to the number of visitors after 1980?

g) What was the least popular attraction in 1986?

h) How did the number of visitors to the museum in 1983 compare with the number of visitors there in 1978?

Unit 20 Comparing things

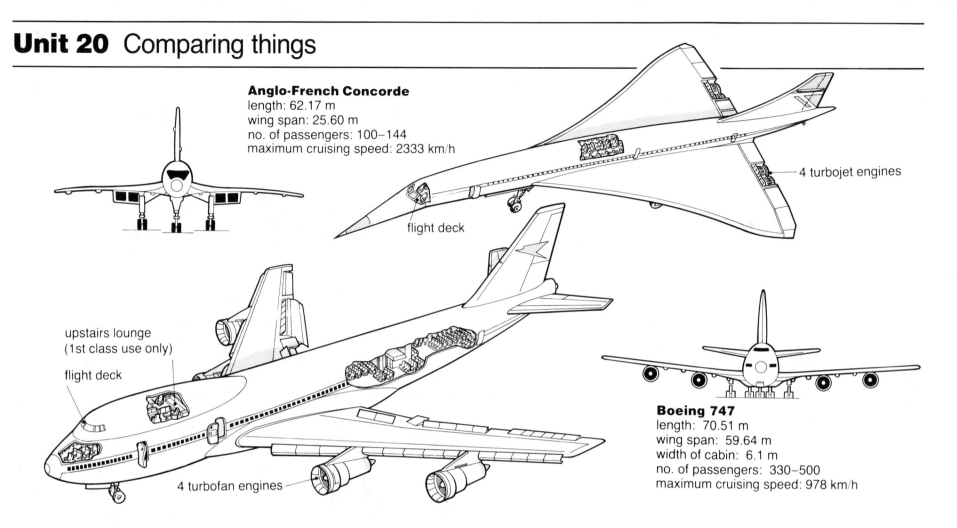

Anglo-French Concorde
length: 62.17 m
wing span: 25.60 m
no. of passengers: 100–144
maximum cruising speed: 2333 km/h

4 turbojet engines

flight deck

upstairs lounge
(1st class use only)

flight deck

4 turbofan engines

Boeing 747
length: 70.51 m
wing span: 59.64 m
width of cabin: 6.1 m
no. of passengers: 330–500
maximum cruising speed: 978 km/h

Comparison

Write out the following paragraphs, choosing the best word in the brackets. The completed paragraphs should compare the Boeing 747 with the Anglo-French Concorde.

The Boeing 747 is the (fastest/oldest/largest) passenger jet airliner in the world. It is over (70/62/60) metres long with a wing (width/length/span) of about 60 metres. Its (carriage/compartment/cabin) is over 6 metres wide, and (capable/able/possible) of taking up to ten seats and two aisles. Its wide body soon (earned/won/awarded) it the name of 'Jumbo Jet'. (In comparison, To compare, For comparing), the Anglo-French Concorde is much thinner and

sleeker (in appearance/to appear/when appearing), with a far (narrow/narrower/narrowest) cabin allowing for only four seats across and (one aisle/two aisles) down the middle. In many other ways too, the Boeing is completely (similar to/different from/identical to) the Concorde. The Concorde, for example, is (smaller than/as small as/as large as) the Boeing 747, its total length (been/being/be) 62 metres and its (tail/flight/wing) span under 26 metres.

The Boeing 747 (takes/accepts/receives) up to 500 passengers (while/when/as) Concorde's normal (volume/capacity/proportion) is 144. Moreover, (different from/contrary to/unlike) the Concorde, the Boeing 747 has a small upstairs lounge. The Boeing's flight (room/deck/office) is

also on the second floor in front of the lounge.

Both aircraft are (like/similar/equivalent) in that they have four powerful engines. However, while there are two turbofan engines at the front of each of the Boeing's wings, there are two turbojet engines at the (front/end/rear) of each of the Concorde's delta-shaped (body/wings/tail). The Concorde's great advantage is its speed. It is capable of flying long distances (by/at/in) supersonic speed. Its maximum cruising speed, for example, is 2,333 km/h, compared with the Boeing 747's 978 km/h. Thus, the Concorde can (double/equal/halve) the time normally (taken/passed/made) for journeys by the Boeing 747 and other conventional aircraft.

20

PTS 150 Hydrofoil
length: 37.9 m
width (maximum beam): 7.5 m
no. of passengers: 250
cruising speed: 67.5 km/h
(36.5 knots)

SR.N4 Mk3 Hovercraft
length: 56.38 m
width (maximum beam): 23.16 m
no. of passengers: 418; cars: 54–60
cruising speed: 110–120 km/h (60–65 knots) – calm sea
                 65–83 km/h (35–45 knots) – rough sea

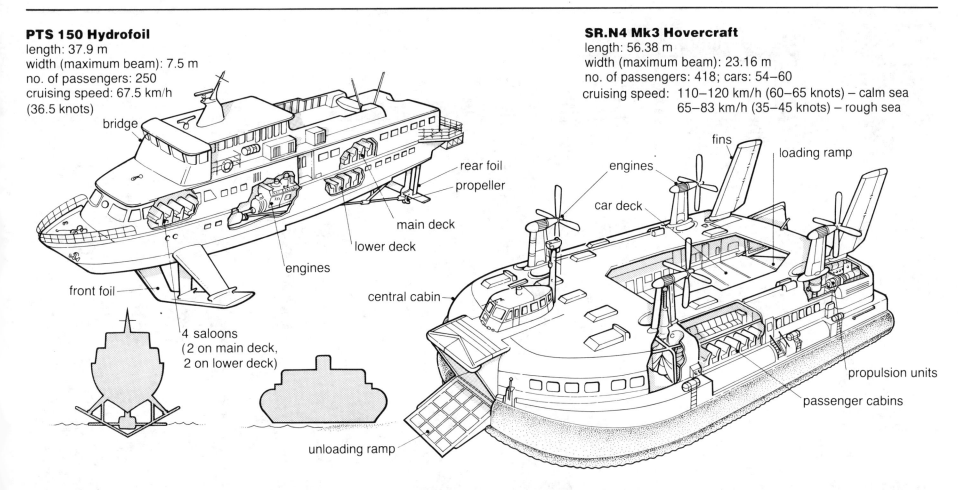

bridge
rear foil
propeller
main deck
lower deck
engines
front foil
4 saloons
(2 on main deck,
2 on lower deck)
unloading ramp

fins
loading ramp
engines
car deck
central cabin
propulsion units
passenger cabins

Vocabulary

craft, hydrofoil, hovercraft, ACV (air cushion vehicle)
dimensions, performance, cruising speed
cabin, (passenger) accommodation, deck, saloon, bridge, ramp
load, unload
foils, (rubber) skirt, air cushion, fins, propellers, propulsion units

Connectives

in comparison with, compared with, too, also, unlike, similar to, different from, while, moreover, however, thus

Questions

Answer these questions about the hydrofoil and the hovercraft in the pictures above.

a) What are the dimensions of the SR.N4 Mark 3 Hovercraft?
b) How much longer is it than the PTS 150 Hydrofoil?
c) How many passengers can the PTS 150 Hydrofoil take?
d) How are they accommodated on the hydrofoil?
e) How many passengers and cars can the SR.N4 Mark 3 Hovercraft carry?
f) Where is the car deck?
g) Where are the engines located on both these craft?
h) Which is faster: the hydrofoil or the hovercraft?
i) How does a hovercraft move?
j) What two advantages do you think the hovercraft has over the hydrofoil?

Writing: 1

Write a short description of the PTS 150 Hydrofoil and the SR.N4 Mark 3 Hovercraft, comparing the two types of craft.

Writing: 2

Consult any appropriate reference books and write a brief comparison of **one** of the following pairs: a submarine and a diving-bell, a canoe and a rowing-boat, a speed-boat and a yacht, a glider and a small aeroplane, or a rocket and a space-shuttle.

Telling a story

Write out the following story about the burglary in the pictures. Choose the best word in brackets.

Linda Shaw was about to (have/put/dine) her evening meal with her parents and grandmother when something rather (afraid/frightening/terrified) happened. The family had just sat down at a table in the (kitchen/dining-room/lounge) and had called Linda's brother Tony to join them when three (arms/armed/arming) men broke (out/off/in). One of the men pointed a gun (to/at/on) them while another (picked/held/threatened) a knife. The family were all terrified, except Tony, who was so (excited/engrossed/attentive) in watching television that he had no idea anything was (wrong/mistaken/incorrect). The men began to put everything that was (worthy/valuable/likeable) into a large (sack/box/case). However, so intent were they on (robbing/catching/stealing) things that they did not see Linda write the word 'HELP' on a piece of paper. The next moment Linda had (dropped/fallen/collapsed) the paper out of the window on to the street below. Soon afterwards two (bystanders/spectators/passers-by) saw it. One of them (picked/chose/selected) it up while the other (glimpsed/glanced/caught sight) up at the window and saw the (shadow/silhouette/shade) of one of the armed men. There was a telephone box nearby and a few minutes later the police were able to (hold/imprison/catch) the armed men red-handed. As the burglars were being taken away, Tony came out of the (lounge/television/building), appearing completely (dumb/excited/bewildered). He had been (watching/attending to/seeing) television throughout the whole (accident/occurrence/incident).

4

5

6

Questions

Answer these questions about the pictures.

a) What do you think the man in the doorway is going to do in Picture 1?
b) What's the woman with the glasses doing?
c) Where are the suspicious-looking men in Picture 2?
d) What's the man at the front of the queue doing in Picture 3?
e) What are his two friends doing?
f) What's the manager doing in Picture 4?
g) How do you think everyone feels except for the woman reading the book?
h) Why are the robbers startled in Picture 5?
i) What's the manager doing in this picture?
j) What's the woman with the glasses doing in Picture 6?
k) What else is happening in this picture?

Writing: 1

Write a short account of what happened in the bank.

Writing: 2

You have read and written stories of a burglary and a bank hold-up. Now write a story about a kidnap, making it as exciting as possible.

Vocabulary

bank, counter, till, desk
cashier, manager
(bank) robbers, gunmen, armed men
suspicious-looking, engrossed in
hold-up, robbery
with his hands up/above his head

terrified, frightened, surprised, amazed, startled, confused, bewildered
alarm button/switch
rob, steal, threaten, demand, snatch, surrender (to the police)
clap, applaud, congratulate, thank

Connectives

when, while, who, that (= which), however, the next moment, soon afterwards, a few minutes later, as, except, so . . . that

Biographical account

Write out the following notes as complete sentences. A single oblique line (/) denotes the end of a short unit in a sentence and a double oblique line (//) denotes the end of a sentence. The completed paragraphs should give a short account of the life of Alexander Graham Bell.

Alexander Graham Bell / inventor of telephone / born Edinburgh 1847 / died 1922// when Bell young man / very ill// long illness / one of chief reasons for parents emigrating Canada// in Canada Bell recovered from illness / began teaching deaf children// so successful / obtained post University of Boston / became professor / result of work in speech and hearing//

Bell began experiment with ways / people communicate over long distances// 1874 succeeded inventing telephone// however, not until 1876 / world's first telephone exhibited publicly// first complete sentence spoken over telephone / 'Mr Watson, come here. I want you'//

Alexander Graham Bell continued experimenting all life// other inventions included new kind of record player / played world's first records / made of wax// later experimented with kites / developed aeroplane certain ways// even helped make hydrofoil.

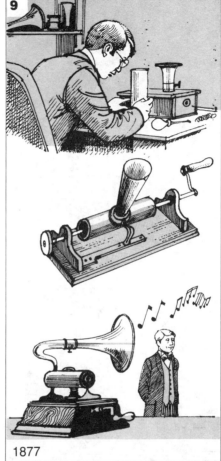

1877

Edison died in 1931

Vocabulary

born, died, dull, backward, curious, impatient
expel,
(grow) vegetables, (buy) chemicals,
(offer) job/post/position,
(sell) magazines
experiment (v), do/conduct
experiments, repair (machine),
succeed in, invent, catch fire
cellar, luggage van, printing press,
(weekly) newspaper, telegraph
office, laboratory, invention,
gramophone, roller-shaped (records),
electric light bulb, street lamp

Connectives

when, so . . . that, however, later

Questions

Answer these questions about the
pictures.

a) When and where was Edison
born?

b) Edison asked so many questions
in school that . . . What
happened?

c) What did his mother do?

d) How did Edison manage to earn
money for his experiments?

e) Where did Edison get his first job
in New York?

f) What did he repair while he was
waiting for his job interview?

g) What did Edison invent in 1877?

h) What else did he invent?

Writing: 1

Write a short biographical account of
the life of Thomas Alva Edison, one
of the world's greatest inventors.

Writing: 2

Now write a short biography of the
life of the historical figure whom you
admire most.

Unit 23 Comparing leisure patterns

Japan

Australia

Comparison

Rewrite the following paragraphs which compare leisure time in Japan with leisure time in Australia. Replace each blank with a suitable word.

It is often difficult to draw conclusions about the various . . 1 . . in which people spend their . . 2 . . in different countries. However, there are several . . 3 . . in leisure patterns between Japan and Australia. For example, most . . 4 . . and . . 5 . . enjoy spending their weekends and holidays on the . . 6 . . , travelling there by car or by train. Hiking, . . 7 . . and . . 8 . . are also popular in both . . 9 . . , though . . 10 . . seems to be more popular in . . 11 . . than in Japan. Most people in Japan and Australia, moreover, like travelling about and . . 12 . . foreign countries. Exercise and sports are very . . 13 . . in both countries. Many excellent sports facilities are provided by private firms in . . 14 . . and by clubs in . . 15 . . .

Whereas many Australians . .^{16}. . drinking . .^{17}. . in their favourite club, most Japanese . .^{18}. . to frequent their favourite coffee bar to taste different blends of . .^{19}. . Moreover, . .^{20}. . the average Australian likes to entertain guests for barbecue parties in his . .^{21}. ., the . .^{22}. . Japanese prefers to . .^{23}. . guests in . .^{24}. . The

. .^{25}. . played in the two countries also . .^{26}. . Baseball and . .^{27}. . are the most popular . .^{28}. . in Japan, but . .^{29}. . and bowls are the most popular . .^{30}. . in Australia. Australians also . .^{31}. . from Japanese in their hobbies. On the whole, Australians are . .^{32}. . on such outdoor . .^{33}. . as . .^{34}. . and all kinds of water sports, while

Japanese usually prefer the more leisurely pastimes of . .^{35}. . arrangement, . .^{36}. . and reading.

China

   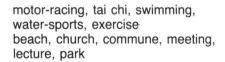

Brazil

Vocabulary

festival, Dragon Boat (Festival), carnival, picnic (read/browse through) newspapers/magazines orchestra, (attend) concert, guitar, music-lover indoor games, chess, table-tennis outdoor games, basketball, football, gambling, sports, horse-racing, motor-racing, tai chi, swimming, water-sports, exercise beach, church, commune, meeting, lecture, park

Connectives

in which, however, for example, *-ing forms*, though, whereas, moreover, also

Questions

Answer these questions about the pictures.

a) How are the activities in China and Brazil similar in Picture 1?
b) What are the people doing in Picture 2 in each case?
c) What do both the Chinese and Brazilians like to read?
d) What hobby do the people in both countries enjoy?
e) In which country are horse-racing and motor-racing very popular?
f) In which country is chess one of the most popular indoor games?
g) What are the two most popular sports in China?

h) What is the national sport of Brazil?

i) Where do people in China and Brazil often enjoy going? What do they do there?

j) In which country do people often go to church in their leisure time?

k) What do you think the people are doing in China in Picture 8?

Writing: 1

Write two paragraphs comparing the ways in which people spend their leisure in China with the ways in which people spend their leisure in Brazil.

Writing: 2

Now compare the ways in which people spend their leisure in your country with the ways people spend their leisure in Japan (or another country of your choice).

Unit 24 Reporting changes

Description

Rewrite the following paragraph describing the room above after the burglary. Put each verb in brackets in its correct form.

Begin: *The window has been broken and there are . . .*

The window (break) and there are pieces of glass on the carpet. One of the curtains (pull down) and the other (tear). Although the lamp and books on the desk (not touch), the typewriter which was there (steal). The drawers of the desk (open) and their contents (scatter) over the floor. The desk chair (overturn) but the other chairs and the sofa (not move). The picture on the wall (tilt) and the glass cabinet under it (damage) when the doors (force) open. All the ornaments in the cabinet (steal), the two vases on the chest (disappear), and the bowl of flowers (knock over), spilling the water on the carpet. Although the records (not touch), the camera which was on the sofa (take). Worst of all, the television (go)!

24

Vocabulary

(detached) house, (adjoining) garage, (garden) hut/shed, drive, fence
flood, damage, injure, tilt, lean, disappear, block,

blow { off / down / over / away }

ambulance, stretcher

Connectives

although, but, which, when, -ing forms

Questions

Answer these questions about the pictures above.

a) What's happened in the second picture?
b) What's been flooded?
c) What's blocking the road?
d) What's happened to the garage roof?
e) What's disappeared?
f) What has happened to the windows of the house?
g) How has the car been damaged?
h) Why has the ambulance come?

Writing: 1

Write a short paragraph about Picture 2, describing the damage caused by the storm.

Writing: 2

Imagine that there has been **either** a fire in a well-known building in your neighbourhood (e.g. a college, a library, a cinema, a hospital), **or** an earthquake. Describe the scene both **before** the event and **after** the event.

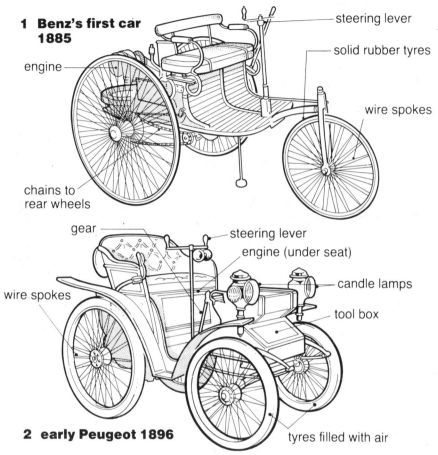

1 Benz's first car 1885

steering lever

engine

solid rubber tyres

wire spokes

chains to rear wheels

gear

steering lever

engine (under seat)

wire spokes

candle lamps

tool box

2 early Peugeot 1896

tyres filled with air

steering wheel

engine

3 Panhard 1902

radiator (made from metal tubes)

chains

petrol tank

wooden wheels

tyres filled with air

brakes (on rear wheels only)

rear seats

front seats

windscreen

bonnet

wings

running board

4 Rolls Royce 1907

Descriptions

Complete the following paragraphs by replacing the blanks with the correct group of words taken from the box. The completed paragraphs trace the history of the motor car by describing four early cars.

---

but also the steering lever on the earlier cars was replaced by a wheel

filled with air

which the driver moved from side to side to steer the car

as well as both front and back seats

one small front wheel and two larger rear wheels

a pair of candle lamps

nevertheless it was an open car and had no front doors

because they were designed like the old horse-drawn carriages

resemble the present-day motor car

the driver and passenger sat

Many of the petrol-driven cars of the 1880s resembled tricycles in certain ways, having ...1... In Benz's first car the engine itself was behind a seat where ...2... In place of the modern steering wheel was a lever ...3... These cars were often referred to as 'horseless' carriages ...4... Although the Peugeot car of 1896 was like a small carriage, its wheels had wire spokes and tyres ...5... At the front, there was a box for tools and ...6... Like the early Benz car, a lever was used to steer the car.

The 1902 Panhard car was one of the first cars to ...7... as its engine was in the front part of the car under a long bonnet. Not only was the engine cooled by a radiator at the front of the car, ...8...

Within a few years, these cars had begun to look far more like the cars we see today. The 1907 Rolls Royce model had a modern-type bonnet ...9... It even had a windscreen, too, but ...10...

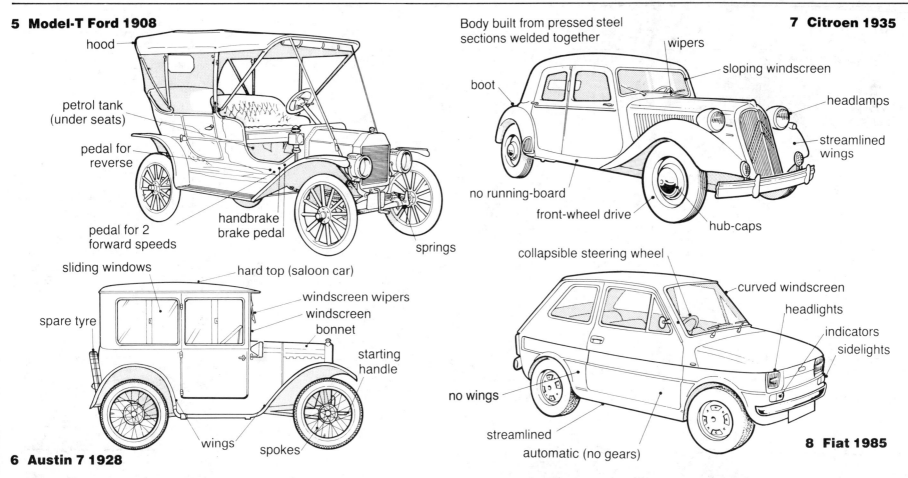

25

5 Model-T Ford 1908

hood

petrol tank (under seats)

pedal for reverse

pedal for 2 forward speeds

handbrake brake pedal

springs

7 Citroen 1935

Body built from pressed steel sections welded together

wipers

boot

sloping windscreen

headlamps

streamlined wings

no running-board

front-wheel drive

hub-caps

sliding windows

hard top (saloon car)

windscreen wipers

windscreen

bonnet

spare tyre

starting handle

wings

spokes

6 Austin 7 1928

collapsible steering wheel

curved windscreen

headlights

indicators

sidelights

no wings

streamlined

automatic (no gears)

8 Fiat 1985

Vocabulary

chassis, body, engine, bonnet (hood), windscreen (windshield), windscreen wiper, boot (trunk), bumpers (fenders), mudguards, running-boards, wings, headlights, sidelights, indicators, (steering) wheel, steering column, brake, clutch, accelerator, dashboard, petrol tank, exhaust (pipe), silencer, (spare) wheel, spokes, tyres, hub-caps pressed steel, streamlined, automatic, saloon (car), sports car

Connectives

which, where, in place of, although, nevertheless, because, like, as, not only . . ., but also, too

Questions

Answer these questions about the pictures above.

a) Which car first appeared in 1908?
b) How was the car made more comfortable?
c) What were the pedals used for?
d) What precautions were taken in case of bad weather?
e) Was the Austin 7 a saloon or a sports car?
f) Why do you think it had sliding windows?
g) Where was the spare tyre kept on this car?
h) How did the Citroen differ basically in shape from the Austin 7?
i) What new feature did this car have at the rear and for what purpose?
j) Were the wings part of the body of the Citroen or separate?
k) Why do you think the car body was built from pressed steel?
l) In what ways does the appearance of the 1985 Fiat differ from the 1934 Citroen?
m) How is it safer?
n) The 1985 Fiat in the picture above is automatic. What is meant by this?

Writing: 1

Write four short paragraphs describing the cars illustrated above. Your paragraphs should form a continuation of the four paragraphs on the previous page, tracing the development of the modern car.

Writing: 2

After consulting any suitable reference books, trace the history and development of one of the following: the aeroplane, the telephone, the modern bicycle, clocks and watches, or the cinema.

Fossil fuels

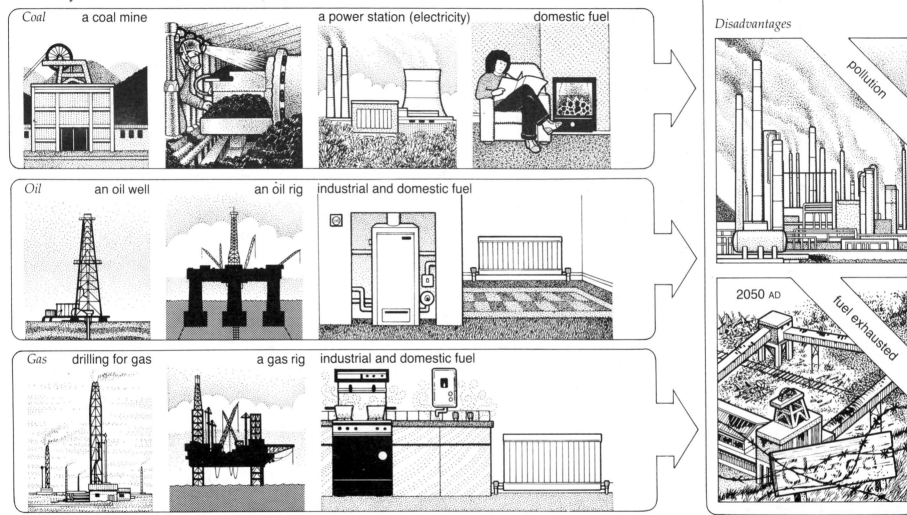

Coal — a coal mine — a power station (electricity) — domestic fuel

Oil — an oil well — an oil rig — industrial and domestic fuel

Gas — drilling for gas — a gas rig — industrial and domestic fuel

Disadvantages — pollution

2050 AD — fuel exhausted

Classification

The information in the pictures will help you to complete the blanks in the following classification of fossil fuels. Write out the paragraph, replacing each blank with one word.

Most conventional sources of . . 1 . . can be divided into . . 2 . . main . . 3 . ., according to the . . 4 . . of fossil fuel used. The first type to be used on a wide scale was . . 5 . ., which is now . . 6 . . at great depths. Formed from decaying trees and plants, . . 7 . . has long been used both for . . 8 . . purposes and in industry. A large number of power . . 9 . . even use coal to . . 10 . . electricity. . . 11 . ., however, has now replaced coal as one of the most important sources of . . 12 . . It is obtained by . . 13 . . deep holes in the earth and . . 14 . . up supplies from large underground reservoirs. Almost half the . . 15 . . used in the world today is provided by oil. Like oil, natural . . 16 . . is obtained by . . 17 . . deep into the earth both on . . 18 . . and sea. On the whole, fossil . . 19 . . are safe to use but they have two important . . 20 . . Not only do they . . 21 . . the environment, but they are not renewable. It is estimated that almost all these . . 22 . . sources will have been . . 23 . . by the middle of the next . . 24 . .

26

Alternative energy sources

hydro-electric power

water-wheel

Geothermal energy

tidal power

wave-power

Disadvantages

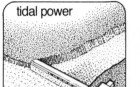

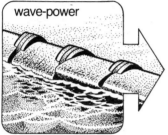

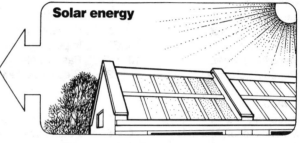

Solar energy

Wind power

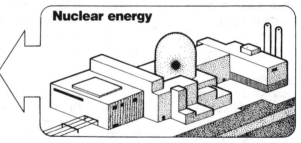

Nuclear energy

Vocabulary

solar energy/power, wind power,
water power, hydro-electric power,
tidal power, wave power, geothermal
energy/power, nuclear energy/power
solar panel, (sun's) rays,
windmill, wind machine, sail, blade,
wind generator, water-wheel,
watermill, (hydro-electric) dam,
(nuclear) power station/plant,
(nuclear) reactor, (nuclear) waste
harness (v)
conversion (into electricity)
hot springs

Connectives

according to, not only . . ., but (also)
which, however, by(-ing), like,
-ed forms

Questions

Answer these questions about the
pictures above.

a) Which form of power requires a
dam?

b) What do you think water-wheels
were used to do?

c) How can energy be obtained from
the sea?

d) How was wind power used in the
past?

e) What other forms of water
power can be used?

f) What are the disadvantages of
wind and wave power?

g) What is geothermal energy?

h) Which do you think would benefit
more from solar energy: the
developed countries or the
developing countries?

i) What is the chief disadvantage of
nuclear energy?

j) What are the advantages of
almost all these forms of energy?

Writing: 1

Write a short paragraph classifying
the different kinds of alternative
energy sources. Describe each
source briefly, using information in
the pictures to help you.

Writing: 2

Now classify **all** the different sources
of energy which could be produced
or obtained in your country. Which
source in your opinion is the best?
Give reasons.

Index

1 List of topics

Answer key

Unit 1
Descriptions
A David Robinson B Penny Green C Mr Carlson

Unit 2
Description
1 at (or in) 2 in 3 from 4 from (or through) 5 of (or in) 6 front 7 with 8 beyond (or behind) 9 of 10 on 11 nearby 12 behind 13 right 14 up 15 in 16 from (or off) 17 middle 18 from 19 at 20 for

Unit 3
Descriptions
Peter Lee – him – him – Peter Lee – tall – of medium build – He – a young-man – his – early twenties – long – swarthy – He – an angular – suspicious – him – he – sloppily – old jeans and a T-shirt – boots – he
Mrs Shaw – her – her – Mrs Shaw – short – stocky – She – an old – woman – her – mid-sixties – frizzy – dark – She – a round – cheerful – her – she – smartly (or well-) – a matching blouse and skirt – high-heeled shoes – she Miss Wilson – her – her – Miss Wilson – of average height – slim – She – a middle-aged – woman – her – late thirties – wavy – fair – She – an attractive – kind – her – she – well (or smartly) – a jumper and slacks – flat shoes – she

Unit 4
Description
A Mr and Mrs Flint get up at quarter to six in the morning, and Mrs Flint makes breakfast for her husband. After breakfast, Mr Flint leaves home to work in the fields nearby. He begins work at half-past six every morning as soon as it is light. He then spends the first part of the morning feeding his calves, and at about nine o'clock he begins to plough the fields with a small, modern tractor.
B Mr and Mrs Flint's three children get up at half-past seven every morning, have their breakfast and then help their mother to wash up. At eight-thirty they set off for school, which is over two miles away. They travel to school by bus every day.
C As soon as the children have left, Mrs Flint feeds the hens and picks up the eggs which they have laid. She makes some tea and sandwiches for her husband. Then she has lunch with him before helping him to work on the farm. She works very hard in the fields until four o'clock.
D When Mrs Flint returns home, her three children help her to prepare the evening meal. Mr Flint returns home at six o'clock, and the family have their evening meal half-an-hour later. After the meal, Mr Flint plants some vegetables, while the children do their homework. Kim, Joe and May go to bed at nine

o'clock, and their parents go to bed an hour and a half later.

Unit 5
Writing notes in full (suggested sentences only)
On Monday we all set off early for High Force Waterfall. We took a lot of photographs and later explored the caves nearby. We were so tired that we spent the following day lying on the beach and swimming a lot. On Wednesday we went shopping for presents and souvenirs. Then in the evening we went to the cinema to see a very exciting film called 'Danger at Midnight'. The next morning we went by train to Orpington Zoo, where we saw some giraffes! Unfortunately, it rained all day on Friday, and so we stayed in the hotel and played table tennis. On the last day of my holidays we got up early and left the hotel at ten o'clock in the morning in good time for the long journey back home.

Unit 6
Telling a story
1 driving 2 road 3 broke 4 but 5 staying 6 until 7 go 8 However 9 agree 10 path 11 lead 12 lost 13 frightened 14 fell 15 arms 16 tree 17 car 18 men 19 walked 20 Bill 21 talking 22 repair

Unit 7
Descriptions (suggested answers only)
Miniature clock: The clock is so small that it can be carried around very conveniently either in a pocket or a handbag. or The clock is not only very attractive in appearance but extremely useful, having an alarm and calendar.
Sports cycle: The sports cycle is very light, and suitable not only for racing but also for touring the countryside. or The sports cycle is extremely well-made and beautifully designed. or Although not much more expensive than an ordinary cycle, the sports cycle has many accessories, including a 10-speed gear, a saddlebag and two lights.
Radio cassette: The radio cassette is light, and can be used anywhere as it operates on both batteries and mains. or This radio cassette is quite small but it is very powerful and gives excellent sound reproduction. or It is possible not only to record from the radio but also to copy tapes.
Briefcase: Although made from real leather, the briefcase is surprisingly cheap. or The briefcase can hold a lot as it is expandable and has large pockets and a pen holder. or It is possible to keep everything safe in the briefcase as it has combination locks.

Unit 8
Description
1 student's answer: between thirteen and sixteen 2 medium/average 3 curly brown/dark (or even brown/dark, curly) 4 skirt/blouse 5 blouse/skirt 6 office 7 mother 8 nurse 9 sister 10 brother 11 typist/secretary 12 Biggen 13 sister, who 14 primary/junior school 15 cousin 16 who 17 class/form/school 18 who 19 school 20 5B 21 history 22 interested 23 history 24 China 25 maths/mathematics/arithmetic 26 become/be 27 favourite 28 swimming 29 table tennis 30 chess 31 sewing/dress-making/photography 32 photography/sewing/dress-making

Unit 9
Descriptions
First paragraph: A 1, B 3, C 2, D 3
Second paragraph: A 2, B 1, C 3, D 1
Third paragraph: A 3, B 2, C 1, D 2

Unit 10
Comparison
larger – circular – whereas – like – grown – west – the north and the south – industrial – linked – rail – fishing – coast – by – on the other hand – resort – industry – which – along – access – beaches – west – east – sailing – Unlike – central – comes from – tourism

Unit 11
Writing a recipe
1 eggs 2 tomatoes 3 onion 4 pepper 5 onion 6 oil 7 tomatoes 8 tomatoes/onion 9 onion/tomatoes 10 eggs 11 bowl 12 tablespoonfuls 13 frying pan 14 onion/tomato 15 tomato/onion 16 frying, verbs: slice, fry, sliced, adding, frying, add, set, Take, beat, Heat, pouring, beaten, put, fold, taking, serve/serving

Unit 12
Report
Next, four teaspoonfuls of washing soda were added and stirred thoroughly until all the washing soda was/had been dissolved. The jar was put in a bowl of very hot water in order to maintain the temperature of the solution in the jar. More washing soda was added, and the stirring was continued/the solution was stirred after each teaspoonful had been added. Washing soda was added until no more dissolved/would dissolve. Next, a paper clip was tied onto a pencil, and the pencil was allowed to rest over the jar with the paper clip suspended in the solution. After a few days the paper clip was covered with crystals.

Unit 13
Directions
1

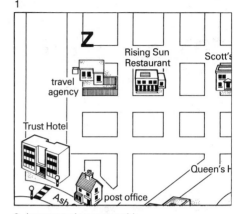

2 (suggested answer only)
Turn left when you leave the writer's house and take the first turning right. Walk down this road and take the fourth turning right into Ash Grove. Walk along Ash Grove, crossing it at the zebra crossing in front of the Trust Hotel. Bear left into Hanover Road and keep straight on until you get to the zebra crossing just after the Street Lane junction. Cross the road here and keep straight on. On your right you will see the new Ford Supermarket and on your left the ABC Cinema. Cross Woodlawn Lane and continue straight on, passing the Bank of Asia on your right and a small park just opposite. When you come to Elm Avenue, turn right. The bus station is in Elm Avenue just after the first turning on the left.

Unit 14
Reports
1 the driver of car A
2 (suggested answer only)
I was driving down a road at a little over 50 km/h when the car in front of me slowed down. I accelerated in order to overtake the car. I then noticed the T-junction in front, but unfortunately there was not enough time to slow down. At that moment a lorry was approaching the T-junction from right to left, travelling at approximately 30 km/h. It was necessary for me to swerve to the left in order to avoid hitting the lorry. However, the car at the side of me prevented me from swerving as much as I wanted, and my car hit the side of the lorry, causing considerable damage to my car. The car which I had tried to overtake mounted the pavement, scraped its front wing against a wall and hit a road sign. I was slightly injured in the accident but fortunately the lorry driver was not hurt. The only other witness was the driver of a sports car which had been approaching the T-junction in the opposite direction to the lorry.

Answer key

Unit 15
Description
5, 10, 8, 2, 6, 3, 11, 1, 9, 4, 7

Unit 16
Description
1 chiefly by heat from the sun, and by the wind. 2 air currents carry most of the moisture over the land. 3 more moisture collects in the air. 4 over cooler air. 5 and begins to cool. 6 and rain clouds form. 7 they fall as rain or snow over the land, especially over the hills. 8 eventually returning to the sea and completing the cycle.

Unit 17
Description
3, 7, 6, 1, 5, 8, 2, 4

Unit 18
Description (*suggested answer only*)
As we walked up the hill, we saw the land fall away on either side. There were a few farms scattered about in the wide valley on our left, but no traces of buildings or fields were visible in the narrow valley on our right. We continued along a high ridge for several miles, before we eventually descended into the narrow valley on our right. There were fewer trees in the valley now, and the ruins of a small hut were visible on the other side of a stream. Before we began to climb again, we crossed a narrow wooden bridge over the stream. A large waterfall towered above us, on the other side of which we could see the route up. After we had walked with great difficulty under the waterfall, we slowly climbed up the rocky face. On the top was a huge plateau which stretched for miles. A solitary tree, stunted and dwarfed, seemed to emphasise the desolation. In the far distance it was possible to make out the faint outline of a mountain.

Unit 19
Description
Sentence 3: 60,000 *Sentence 4*: decreased/fell/dropped; slowly/gradually/steadily; rose/climbed/increased; steadily *Sentence 5*: sharp/steep/sudden; increase/rise/climb; 70,000; 95,000 *Sentence 6*: rose/increased/climbed; (*approx*) 48,000 (*approx*) 64,000; fell/decreased/dropped; steadily; (*approx*) 45,000 *Sentence 7*: (*approx*) 26,000 *Sentence 8*: rose/increased/climbed; slightly; rose/increased/climbed; sharply/suddenly/steeply *Sentence 9*: levelled off; steady

Unit 20
Comparison
largest – 70 – span – cabin – capable – earned – In comparison – in appearance – narrower – one aisle – different from – smaller than – being – wing – takes – while – capacity – unlike –

deck – similar – rear – wings – at – halve – taken

Unit 21
Telling a story
have – frightening – dining-room – armed – in – at – held – engrossed – wrong – valuable – sack – stealing – dropped – passers-by – picked – glanced – silhouette – catch – lounge – bewildered – watching – incident

Unit 22
Biographical account (*suggested answer only*)
Alexander Graham Bell, the inventor of the telephone, was born in Edinburgh in 1847 and died in 1922. When Bell was a young man, he was very ill. Indeed, his long illness was one of the chief reasons for his parents emigrating to Canada. In Canada, Bell eventually recovered from his illness and began teaching deaf children. He was so successful that he obtained a post at the University of Boston, where he became a professor as a result of his work in speech and hearing.

Bell began to experiment with ways in which people could communicate over long distances. In 1874 he succeeded in inventing the telephone. However, it was not until 1876 that the world's first telephone was exhibited publicly. The first complete sentence ever spoken over the telephone was 'Mr Watson, come here. I want you.'

Alexander Graham Bell continued experimenting all his life. His other inventions included a new kind of record player which played the world's first records made of wax. Later, he experimented with kites and developed the aeroplane in certain ways. He even helped to make a hydrofoil.

Unit 23
Comparison
1 ways 2 leisure/free time/spare time
3 similarities 4 Japanese/Australians
5 Australians/Japanese 6 beach
7 climbing/fishing 8 fishing/climbing
9 countries 10 camping 11 Australia
12 visiting/touring 13 popular/common
14 Japan 15 Australia 16 like/enjoy
17 beer 18 like 19 coffee
20 although/whereas/while
21 home/house/garden 22 average
23 entertain/take 24 restaurants 25 games
26 differ 27 wrestling 28 sports
29 cricket 30 games/sports 31 differ
32 keen 33 hobbies/activities
34 gardening 35 flower 36 painting

Unit 24
Description
has been broken, has been pulled down, (has been) torn, have not been touched, has been stolen, have been opened, (have been)

scattered, has been overturned, have not been moved, has been tilted, was damaged, were forced, have been stolen, have disappeared, has been knocked over, have not been touched, has been taken, has gone

Unit 25
Descriptions
1 one small front wheel and two larger rear wheels 2 the driver and passenger sat
3 which the driver moved from side to side to steer the car 4 because they were designed like the old horse-drawn carriages 5 filled with air 6 a pair of candle lamps
7 resemble the present-day motor car 8 but also the steering lever on the earlier cars was replaced by a wheel 9 as well as both front and back seats 10 nevertheless it was an open car and had no front doors.

Unit 26
Classification
1 energy 2 three
3 kinds/types/forms/categories
4 type/kind/sort 5 coal 6 mined/dug
7 coal 8 domestic 9 stations
10 produce/generate/make 11 Oil
12 energy 13 drilling 14 pumping
15 energy 16 gas 17 drilling 18 land
19 fuels 20 drawbacks/disadvantages
21 pollute/spoil
22 three/conventional/fuel/energy
23 exhausted/used 24 century